Dearei

Conquering The Impossible:
Making The Dream Come True

By

Carol Higgins

*Dream it
Believe it
Achieve it...*

*Love and best wishes
Carol
xxx.*

Copyright © 2015 Carol Higgins

Carol Higgins is hereby identified as the sole author of the entire works herein and reserves all of her rights to be identified as such and does not give permission for any of this material to be used for advertising purposes. However, short paragraphs totalling no more than 200 words may be used for educational or review purposes.

ISBN:9781511624633

ISBN-13

DEDICATION

For my beautiful sister Donna, son Jake & daughter Ella.

African Trilogy

Part 1 – My Climb To The Summit Of Mount Kilimanjaro

Part 2 – Making The Dream Come True

Part 3 – My Safari: Another Dream Come True

ACKNOWLEDGMENTS

Thank you to Graham Geddes for the countless hours, days, weeks and months you have spent with me typing, arranging and helping to create this book.

Lisa Thorn for proof reading and dedicating her time to help me make this book possible.

Sue Chater, for believing in me, inspiring my confidence and teaching me how to become a writer.

Northern College, for helping me to learn and grow as a writer.

Liam Rodgers of UpScribe Social Publishing and Author of Dog Knife for support, and advice. Proof reading and editing.

Raphael Achache for the book's front and back cover lay out.

Ella & Jake for listening to me reading it out loud and laughing and crying at all the right moments and inspiring me to carry on.

Jeremy Clark and his son Henry, for early printed proof reads and teas and coffees

Gail Powell, for editorial advice.

Star, for your encouragement, keeping me fed and watered in the countless hours proof reading.

Andrej for inserting pictures and captions at late notice.

Stuart for his loving support.

Joris and Sabina for providing me with a haven to create my book and heal on their beautiful Campsite Laneside.

PROLOGUE

"PEACE TO THE WORLD, I AM A CHAMPION!" I shouted with exhilaration and fulfilment, as I stood on the summit of Mount Kilimanjaro, having just completed my awesome adventure and feat of pure endurance.

As a child I was always surrounded by violence and fear and every time I pulled the dried out wishbone from the chicken after Sunday dinner, I would wish for "peace to the world." I still wish for the same.

PART 1

My Climb To The Summit Of Mount Kilimanjaro

Day 1

14th Feb 2014

My journey began at Leeds & Bradford airport with Steve1, the founder of The Laila Milly Foundation - my chosen charity - and his best friend, also called Steve. By chance, I bumped into a man called James at the airport, who I discovered was also going to be part of our group of eight climbers.

It was so windy, the plane shook nearly all the way to London. However, after two glasses of red wine and listening to great tunes on my mp4 player, which I had just bought from a cash exchange shop for £20, I was buzzing and not even the thought of the plane crashing could dampen my spirit or spoil my anticipation of the adventure ahead.

We arrived at the hotel in Heathrow at 5pm. The room was modern, warm and I had what was going to be my last bath for two weeks! At 7pm we met our guide, Matt, for dinner. Matt was going to navigate our safe passage up Mount Kilamanjiro. There were two Steve's, James, Matt and myself.

The food was mouth-watering, with three courses; a prawn starter, steak and chips followed by cheesecake with a delicious cherry and strawberry topping, and two glasses of red wine.

That's four I've had today. I'd better take it easy, if I am going to be hydrated enough to get up the mountain.

Steve1 was acting strange tonight at dinner, rather distant and not making eye contact. I asked him for a knock at three in the morning (because my phone is an old brick and unreliable after losing my other one whilst skiing on the snow slopes).

He replied, "I can't, but Steve2 can."

I found this disappointing and negative.

I'm already missing my two children, Ella and Jake and also my boyfriend, Stuart. Only two weeks to go before I see them again. Off to sleep now, I am up at 3am to catch a plane to Amsterdam followed by a connecting flight to Tanzania. We should arrive at 9pm tomorrow evening.

Day 2

15th Feb 2014

Stuart called to wake me up at 3am so I could set off in a taxi to the airport at 3.45am. Unfortunately, when we got there, our flight to Amsterdam had been cancelled, due to adverse weather conditions.

I couldn't believe it. I knew immediately this would have a knock-on effect to our itinerary. The flight was rescheduled to 6.45am the next morning.

We met Ying Ying, a Chinese lady, at the airport, who was part of our group. Steve1 commented, saying Ying Ying was going to be the leader and the strong one, in his eyes. He decided this because she had argued herself into flying with us on the rescheduled flight to Amsterdam, rather than being put on a separate flight. Ying Ying lived nearby and went home but we had to book into a budget hotel.

It was a small, cold, clinical looking room and I spent a disappointing day in it because the cancellation meant we couldn't catch our connecting flight to Tanzania.

In the evening, Ying Ying and her family picked us up and we went to the oldest free-standing pub in England for a meal. The meal helped to pass time and Ying Ying's family insisted on paying for everyone's food, which I thought was very kind. We sat around a

Tudor period table, which reminded me of King Arthur and The Round Table. It was magnificent and full of history. It was a pleasant evening. Ying Ying's children enjoyed listening to my stories of deep-sea scuba diving, skiing, sky-diving, co-piloting, camping and vagabonding around the world. I mentioned I did it alone and sometimes with my own kids.

Yes, I had quite a bit to say!

It was amazing when Ying Ying told me that I inspired her children to travel and to explore and experience the adventures that life has to offer.

I looked forward to once again getting up at 3am to catch the 6.45am plane to Amsterdam.

Day 3

16th Feb 2014

Arrived at the airport early in the morning, got on the plane. SUCCESS!

...Until we arrived in Amsterdam and were told the plane to Tanzania was over-booked by eleven people. Steve1 tried to get us on the plane by arguing with the staff and so did I, to no avail. The desk manager was nervously laughing, so I shouted at her with tears in my eyes: "I'm not laughing!"

I felt helpless seeing my dream challenge going through the window.

With two flights cancelled, K.L.M. Airlines gave us each 600 Euros plus 40 Euros in food vouchers. To me, the money was not important as I just wanted to climb Kilimanjaro.

Everyone was on the flight to Tanzania, except both Steve's and me. We were discussing aborting the whole operation because there would not be enough time to acclimatise to the altitude if we delayed any longer. We knew our health could be at stake.

Around this time, the flight manager agreed to place us on another flight at 8:40pm to Nairobi and we decided to take the risk.

I called our guide Matt, who was on the plane, and had a go at him for not letting me fly instead of him and leaving me with two grumps, when two ladies could have gone together. *A bit like on the Titanic...Women first!* I thought. Matt put the phone down on me. I'm sure he will say he lost connection after the line went dead.

> *It can't get any worse! All these flights cancelled, running out of time, not enough time to acclimatise. We need to set off* ***NOW!***

All that time wasted at the airport, I was tired and fed up of waiting around.

With the compensation money, I treated myself to a three course meal and decided, at 1.30pm, to book into the Yotel in the airport for four hours. I could only sleep for two, but still, it was a chilled out space at only 45 Euro. It was like being in a space capsule, all white and clinical with a sink, toilet and bed. Rows of these rooms along narrow corridors are available to nap in. You can see the beds through some of the windows, reminding me of the brothel windows in Amsterdam, although without the prostitute, of course! After I awoke, I ate a McDonald's to refuel and sat having small talk with the Steves.

7pm and I am still waiting in the airport lounge to board at 8.45pm. Hope this flight and the connecting one from Nairobi take us to Kilimanjaro and glad I have my diary and book, Labyrinth by Kate Mosse, to occupy me.

We boarded on time for the nine hour flight but I was separated from the Steves on the plane. I didn't sleep a wink but watched a strange, sad film called, *The Butterfly Effect,* about how every time something good happened, correspondingly something bad did. The film moved me.

"I was grateful for the chilled out space in the Yotel in Amsterdam."

Setting off from Amsterdam for the 9 hour flight to Nairobi.

Welcome to the promised land

I drank plenty of water, asking the flight attendants for the two-litre bottles they were pouring from and after I had drunk two, they would only serve me it by the cup! (I didn't know until we got off the plane, that the guys had been a few rows behind, laughing at me). I ate on the plane, knowing I had to refuel to boost my energy as there would no longer be time for preparation at the hotel because of the delays, as had been planned. We would be going straight to the mountain without proper rest.

Day 4

17th Feb 2014

Landed in Nairobi at 7.15am.

It's raining but quite warm. The airport is old fashioned, tiny and very busy and crammed with people. I am now waiting for my flight to Kilimanjaro airport. I feel a little unnerved at the seriousness of the crowds of people, who looked sweaty, hot and bothered.

After one hour, we caught our flight to Kilimanjaro. The process of applying for the visas when we arrived was funny in itself because the African guard in the airport came and took me out of the queue straight to the front desk. It made me think, this is alright, but what does he want? It was nothing, he was just being kind, and had probably seen how knackered and confused I looked. A wonderful welcome to their beautiful country! Once we had our visas, I was happy to meet up with all the other trekkers I'd been separated from. We had a long drive to the weighing-in gates, then on to the starting point of our climb.

I loved travelling to the starting point, watching the African people and seeing how they thrived off the rich, red land that provides coffee beans, fruit and vegetables. Dotted around the surrounding vast jungle and mountains, people worked their crops relentlessly, planting in-between other plants. This reminded me of permaculture.

I "tatey-picked" in the fields as a child, turnips, cabbages and other crops as well and I would harvest them in the summer months or autumn chill. I plucked pheasant, pigeon and skinned rabbits as I had been shown by my dad how to survive off the land. If I had a penny for every bird I plucked, I'd be rich!

The African sights reminded me of childhood days and inner hunter-gatherer spirit instilled in me from an early age. Everything is done by machines at home now but it did make me wonder, *are we really such different tribes?*

During the drive I occasionally saw cattle and goats being herded along the roadside by a man or a boy waving a stick, directing them to where they were going. I didn't see any clothes shops but lots of markets and many people gathered on the roadside, selling second-hand clothes, footwear, food and furniture. I saw scrap-yards, bars, cafes, other businesses and more. People lined the palm-treed streets, women chatting with babies strapped to their backs, wearing beautiful, bright-coloured clothes, looking happy, relaxed and seemingly enjoying the simple things in life. However, I could see from the hot conditions and the apparent unemployment of so many, that life was hard. Even though there seemed to be enough food and clothes to satisfy their basic needs, I couldn't imagine living that way on a long term basis.

Many of the people I saw were living in square, concrete sheds and huts, with corrugated tin roofs or in small, white bungalows which lined the roads, with no pavements. In parts, sewage flowed openly, attracting swarms of flies and stray dogs, which roamed freely. I was surprised to see motorbikes passing with the whole family sat on them, balancing bundles or pots on their heads whilst speeding along the dry, dusty road. Goodness knows how they did this, I was amazed. People were lovely; there was beautiful clear sunshine and rich lush greenery everywhere.

Tanzania is a country of contrasts. Not all of the homes were as basic along the route, there were many larger white houses and gardens which were clearly owned by more affluent people and many had luxury cars.

Gradually, Mount Kilimanjaro came into view and I began to understand why it is called, "The Mountain of

Greatness."

It was breath-taking.

We drove over mostly rough ground to the weighing-in gates, where they weighed our Jagged Globe bags, to ensure the porters wouldn't be carrying too much. 15kg was our allowance.

I had 20kg, so I had to leave all of my luxuries behind.

It was a nightmare sorting through my luggage and deciding what I would really need. I tried to hide behind the Land Rover whilst carrying out this embarrassing task but everyone could see me; even my knickers fell out onto the mountain side. 5kg had to go back to my hotel along with my other bag, ready for the safari, which I had arranged for after my climb. I had to stuff it all in my other holdall. No shampoo or a towel for 8 days. **Coffees, sweets, posh underwear, lotions, make- up. Everything gone! I would be roughing it for the next 8 days. It wasn't until later I discovered that, in the panic, I had forgotten my hand towel.**

We had to wait for two hours whilst other climbers had their bags weighed and for Matt to get the Government's permission to go on the mountain.

Finally we set off. We drove as near to the foot of Mount Kilimanjaro as possible but the roads became too muddy to continue and the Land Rovers were nearly tipping over. The driver had to let us out at 5pm, nearly two hours walk away from the start of the climb. From then on, it was all on foot to get to the base of Kilimanjaro, where we would take the Lemosho route up the mountain.

We trekked through the jungle with just our head torches to light the way, stumbling over tree roots and rocks. I saw black and white monkeys on the way, probably the size of me and small black monkeys swinging in the trees, like in a Tarzan film. The rain forest was full of noise and not knowing what owned it made it a bit scary. The stars were close and bright above the tall trees. It wasn't until 10.30 pm when we reached our first base camp, at 2800 meters. We had been climbing over rough ground for six hours when we walked into Mti Mkubwa, which means 'Big Tree'. The porters had put up a mess tent for our group of eight people to eat a fantastic home cooked dinner.

Mti Mkubwa – 2750m/9020ft

I was surprised to see lots of other tents already pitched, belonging to other groups of climbers and I felt excited about my expedition ahead, even though I was exhausted.

> *My feet, legs and lower tummy are aching and painful, even though I used my walking poles to take the weight off my lower abdomen. I have had five operations*

The Land Rover dropped us off before the starting point to my climb to take the Lemosho route.

in total in this part of my body. My last surgeon said they could have left a zip in it! All the same, I am sure that after taking painkillers and after a good night's sleep in the two man tent, which I am sharing with Ying Ying, I will be ready to start the eight hour climb in the morning,

Good night x.

Day 5

18th Feb 2014

I woke at 6.30am but wasn't leaving first base until 8.15am. The camp was still asleep so I walked around with my camera, filming everything and everyone I could see, drinking in all my surroundings. It all looked different in the daylight and I couldn't quite believe I was actually in the jungle, another experience I had always wanted to have. I made myself a cuppa and soon afterwards everyone was up and about, getting washed and dressed before breakfast. We had porridge made with maize and water, fruit and a fry-up, coffee and juice. After breakfast there was a briefing about altitude sickness and what we needed to carry that day. I packed my belongings inside my tent so the porters could take it down to carry it to the next camp, which is at 3500m.

I feel quite emotional writing this now. Maybe it is because I am tired. Also it was hard sleeping and getting comfy on the cold, damp, red, mountain earth. Nevertheless, the African guides that we meet are amazingly kind and friendly and I feel humbled by their beautiful spirit and kind nature, as they help us make this climb possible.

Shira One – 3,800m/12,470ft

This was our second camp and I climbed eight hours through more dense jungle with a heavy army rucksack on my back. I have learnt to be first into camp to bag the best tent location and I run my hands across the tent floor to get the least bumpy side. The Chinese have space-age roll up mats and mine is an old, thin, foam one. I could see Kilimanjaro's summit covered in snow when the clouds moved away, *this is what I would be climbing.* Another emotional moment, my dream coming true!

Its dinner time now at 7pm and the smells coming into my tent from the beautifully home-cooked food are delightful. I've just heard that for starters its home-made leek soup, chicken curry, rice, vegetables and sweet pancakes and hot chocolate – yummy!

I took lots of pictures of the stunning mountain and the colourful plants, flowers and other wildlife today, enjoying every breath-taking moment and getting to

The jungle was full of wild plantation and flowers.

The monkeys were swinging from trees.

I was amazed at how they did this.

know our guides and climbers. I watched the Africans carry our belongings on their backs and balancing tents and bags on their heads. I was surprised at how they make this look so easy.

> *Just got to tell you that all I've done this trip is fart. I fart up the mountain and when I am at camp. Eating dinner is a nightmare because I am holding them in. Sharing a tent is embarrassing to me because Ying Ying has to put her neck scarf round her nose, but says nothing! I just went to the porta-loo and farted loud for three minutes and all the camp could hear. What's up with me!* (The combination of surgery and altitude pressure is causing the problem).

Most of the team of eight are supportive of each other. Today I was so cold and wet that my fingers had pins and needles, so James rubbed them and showed me some rotating wrist exercises to get them warm. Also, I was getting head-achey with altitude and he showed me a breathing technique that made it go away. James's brother is a doctor who showed him what to do to encourage the body to produce more red blood cells which help alleviate altitude sickness.

My first few days in Africa have been mixed, starting in the jungle; then up the rocky mountain with the tallest bushes I've ever seen and lots of beautiful

Embarrassing! The porter loo I farted in for three minutes and all the camp could hear.

Our Donna is with me.

Where we ate for eight days.

Porters prepared our dinners everyday.

flowers; then onto the rocky plains. All the time we were surrounded by mountains and then the biggest by far up in the clouds, the summit of the one we are all climbing. Didn't see any animals today though. It has rained nearly all day and most of my gear got wet because I had forgotten to put my clothes and sleeping sack in plastic bags and the zip was leaking. The porters and cooks helped me to dry them over the cooking fire in a small green tent and I hung the rest in the sun. I have been given enough bags to cover everything tomorrow.

> *I am all cosy in my tent now after dinner but want to fart again and Ying Ying is on her way. They stink! Never mind, I am dry and sleepy now, so good night.*
>
> *I miss my family ...*

Day 6

19th Feb 2014

Shira Two – 3,900m/12,675ft

Same routine: up at 6.30am, get packed up and breakfast. This always takes so long because Ying Ying has OCD (Obsessive compulsive disorder) and her stuff is all over the tent, taking her ages to get organized. She even sets the alarm clock an hour early, waking me up at 5.30am, too. Ying Ying has brought everything but the kitchen sink and has hired an extra porter to carry her bags. She even pays them to wipe the toilet seat clean and puts a scarf round her face when she goes. She struggles to stay calm if I splash a drop of tea in our tent! She has a nanny and a cleaner at home and is used to having most chores done for her. She tells me she is married to a rich man who pays for everything and expects her to be the little woman. Not for me!

We walked a short five hours today but I admit it felt more like eight. I was tired of waking up in the night and rising early. Luckily today we walked over flat plains. As usual, the porters carried our camp on their heads and set up before we arrived. It feels like first class camping, like a scene from *George of the Jungle*.

Reg, I call him Captain Reginald, was our guide up the mountain today. I walked with him and he told me of how he has to work hard to pay for his children's education so that they too can get work and earn enough money to live.

Kilimanjaro is more beautiful than I imagined. Today there has been increasingly less vegetation and it is becoming quite barren on the vast plains. The air is too thin for much plant-life to survive. I kept seeing rocks stacked up on top of each other. I have seen this in Hebden Bridge in Yorkshire and people build them to signify that balance is harmony and harmony is balance. Just as Reg was taking a picture of me, a little bird came out of nowhere and perched itself on the top of the small monument. At that moment I felt my sister

Donna's s loving presence, sensing she was taking care of me. Donna has passed over and I felt moved as I remembered her and smiled to myself.

Only four of us did the five hour climb, passed Lava Tower and descending into Baranco, with the others choosing to climb for six hours on a different route. I was glad I didn't go with them because there was a hailstorm just after we got into camp. The hailstones were the size of peas, hurting my hands as I was filming our arrival.

> *We arrived at Baranco at roughly 1.30pm and I can hear the birds singing outside my tent. Some I've never seen before and I am in wonder as their dazzling beauty catches my eye.*
>
> *It has taken me days to climb to the same height from which I did both sky dives. Then it took only twenty minutes to reach altitude and only seven minutes to descend. It blows my mind living up here in the clouds and I know I have much further to go.*
>
> *The thunder is very loud as I write this. I feel full up from lunch, having eaten home-made soup, cheese toasties and mushrooms in pancakes. I eat bananas which are small, compared to ours at*

home and sweet oranges that have green skins and look like giant limes. There is always good food and cups of tea to drink with friends in our mess tent. The chatter is always full of enthusiasm and warmth. I know I mention food and drink a lot, but it is important to keep hydrated and maintain energy levels.

Some people have had to be taken off the mountain today in white rescue Land Rovers and a lady came down with her guide suffering with altitude sickness. I hope this won't happen to me and I can make it to the top. I can see the summit getting closer when the clouds lift and it looks like thick icing dripping down a cake. Maybe I will reach it tomorrow teatime!

Oh My God! We are so high up in the clouds and I cannot believe how loud this thunder is but no one is bothered by it. I'm not either because there is no lightning. If there was, it would be a different story and I would be pooing my pants by now!

I haven't spoken to anyone back home yet and every time I think of Jake and Ella I want to cry, but hold back. You are my

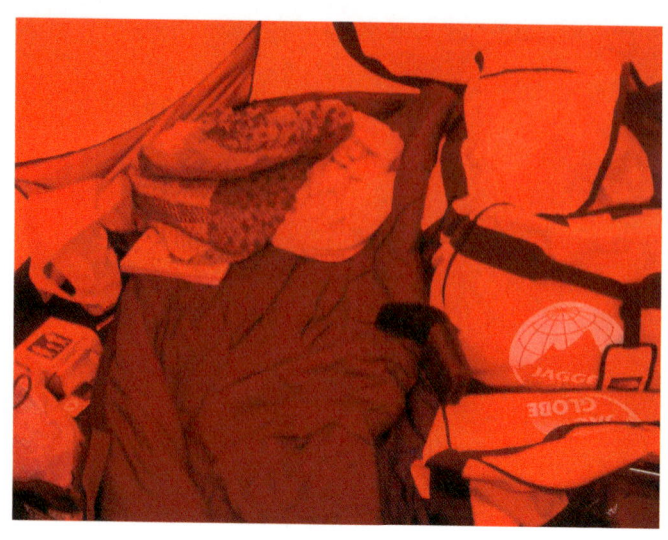

My personal space.

The sky was my home for eight days.

babies and I miss you so much and hope you are safe and well. I keep looking at your pictures and, as usual, can't believe how lucky I am to have such beautiful teenagers of whom I am so proud. Oops, I'm trumping again. I can see you two shaking your heads, laughing, "she's always at it!"

I can't wait to climb high tomorrow. I just took two more strong tablets for my pain and slight headache that won't go away. My eyes are tired and I thought I saw a furry caterpillar moving today but it was a stick, so I am hallucinating slightly too. I'm going to treat myself to a siesta now, seeing as we arrived early. It's not quiet but I am happy to listen to the chatter of everyone.

After a short nap I awoke to the smell of evening meal being cooked. Ying Ying came into the tent. We chatted about her life. She brags about having everything she wants. She has never camped or climbed in her life and thinks this trip will change her OCD - I have my doubts. We chatted about her sending her kids to boarding school to make them independent.

She said, "I have done my job."

I replied, "You can teach children independence

without sending them away."

She said, "I can't teach them independence because I do too much for them."

We obviously have different views on parenting. During our conversation she sprayed Deep Heat and Deodorant. I opened the tent flap and asked her not to as the fumes were getting in my mouth and throat. The look she gave me!

I sat on the rocks watching over the camp, drinking a taste of back home, before the evening meal. It was lovely watching the sun going down after the day's storm.

> *I was watching the comings-and-goings of the camp this evening and I saw Steve1 walking towards the Chinese girls. He saw Celine and was asking how she felt. Celine, Ying Ying and Lisa had been chatting to each other in Chinese for most of the trip, making me feel isolated. I was observing from a distance and I heard Steve1 talking to Ying Ying*
>
> *"What do you think to Carol, do you think she's crazy?" he asked.*
>
> *"Yes, she is crazy!" replied Ying Ying.*
>
> *Then Steve1 said, "Why do you think I'm*

keeping my distance?"

Suddenly it became clear why Steve1 hadn't wanted to give me a wakeup call. They didn't know I could hear.

I shouted over, "I heard that!"

Steve1 skulked away with his head down and started whispering to Steve2 about what happened. I don't feel that I have done anything wrong or crazy and am now upset and angry. I am the only one who has worked hard and against adversity to help raise money and bring awareness to their charity. I have raised £2650 by doing the climb. When she came back to the tent, I asked Ying Ying why she thought I was crazy.

"Sorry, I overreacted," she replied.

I am sorry to say that in the heat of the moment I told her a few home truths about what I thought of her and she left the tent. I think Steve1 is being two-faced and I feel very disappointed. I have lost my trust in him and I am going to keep myself to myself from now on. I am shaking whilst writing this, my karma has been destroyed and he has split the group. I still have to eat and climb with him every day. Shame on his shallow nature!

Well that was an interesting dinner! You could cut the atmosphere with a knife.

In the airport Steve1 spoke behind Matt's back, saying he hadn't got an ounce of male testosterone in him. When the dinner came tonight, soup, vegetables, pasta and beef, I couldn't help myself say that the beef might have some male testosterone in it for anyone who needs it! Actually I was referring to Steves1's own lack of testosterone, because of his bitchiness. Steve's red face was a picture and deadly serious because he thought I might spill the beans about his back-stabbing of Matt. Steve1 was not the only person who had been upsetting people today. Ying Ying had also upset an American lady on the mountain.

"Look at her! Can you believe she's wearing make-up?" she said, pointing at the woman.

"Don't you know it's rude to comment on other people's appearance?" asked the American lady, who was clearly hurt by this.

Ying Ying became defensive and called her

a stupid woman. It just goes to show what Ying Ying and Steve1 are really like. They go about hurting people's feelings because they regard themselves as superior and try to make out it's the other person at fault. Dear me!

I am in bed now it's 7.30pm. I have to be up at 5.30am to climb to 4800m, only to descend to 3900m to sleep. It's a shame to climb to that height only to have to go back down but it's all about acclimatisation.

Ying Ying is moving out tonight. She came in the tent and dragged her stuff out quicker than I could say Jack Flash. Her friends are in the next tent to me and it's a two-man tent like mine. I wonder how she will fit all her stuff in. She said in the beginning if I wasn't in the tent she would be scared to sleep by herself and would sleep with her friends; luckily I like having a tent to myself and I will be able to get ready quicker in the mornings. Steve1 actually caused this. Well done Steve!

Guess what? It's 9pm and I now have a new room-mate. It's Celine, Ying Ying's friend. I like her; she is younger, looks attractive and is chatty, even though her

English is limited.

I have been standing outside the tent drinking hot chocolate, chatting to James, whilst Celine moves in. The stars are bright and beautiful and you can see the Milky Way clearly. As I looked up I could feel the connection to Jake and Ella because the Bear, Orion and the Big Dipper can be seen at home as well. I feel comforted by this.

I've finished my hot chocolate and now it's time for bed.

Miss you all lots, Goodnight Jake, Ella

Day 7

20th Feb 2014

Barranco - 3976m/12,930ft

Its 5.30am and finally morning has arrived. I didn't sleep a wink, it's all part of the altitude sickness, not many are sleeping well. It was a horrible night lying here awake on the cold, hard rock in pain with only a thin foam mat to separate me from the clutches of the freezing mountain. I am wearing as many layers of clothing as I can. If I put any more on, I won't be able to fit in my sleeping bag. At one point I was hallucinating, I saw a black shadow creeping towards my right shoulder and thought the Devil was coming to take me. I nearly had a panic attack but managed to calm myself. Still, it felt so real, I have never experienced anything like it. My mind was all over the place with negative thoughts of what Steve1 had said. I was trying to think of home and my children, positive memories, but my heart kept pounding with anxiety. I have packed up, as always, in the dark with my head torch. Kneeling hurts and, because it's squashed, it is painful and awkward to move about. Also, not having contact with my family is hurting when everyone else is able to contact their loved ones; the battery in my old brick of a phone died before I could get a signal.

I began the day tired and upset, thinking I'd never make the eight hour climb ahead of us. I spoke to Matt in tears and he tried to reassure me not to worry about what Steve1 had said, even though he had brought a negative vibe into the camp and really unsettled me. I told him about the cancer for the first time. I explained that nine months earlier on the 23rd April I had been diagnosed with bowel cancer. They had operated on the

29th May and the major surgery had been to remove a tumour as big as an orange in my colon. During the nine hour operation they took away 23cm of my bowel and re-joined it, bringing the tumour out through my vaginal wall. I had incisions for tubes and cameras all over my stomach and some have not healed without leaving nerve damage.

I was feeling vulnerable and I hadn't told my insurance company about my trip either, it would have cost too much money. I was starting to worry that something would go wrong. I ached with pain and cold and was struggling to breathe, which made me more fatigued. I was getting light nose bleeds, lots of headaches, feeling weepy and wasn't sure if my body would make it.

Matt suggested I shouldn't be on the climb but I told him my surgeon had given me the all-clear for fitness, although it was too early to give me the all-clear for cancer. I didn't tell Matt about the pain from my hernia operation that had gone wrong just a year ago, nor that I was about to have a re-op on it when I got home. I was afraid he wouldn't let me go on. I had been working so hard to try and get my fitness level back up. I had been walking up and down in the pool at my gym four times a week. Then I had progressed to swimming and all the time I was taking pain killers. Then only a year later, I had to go through the same process again after my cancer operation. I walked a lot and swam in the sea and rivers, slowly progressing with Jeremy (my personal trainer and best friend). We also climbed mountains like Catbells and others in the Lake District and the Yorkshire Dales. After talking to Matt, though, I realised there was no way I wasn't going to climb my mountain and with gritted teeth and determination I got up and carried on.

There was an awful atmosphere at breakfast.

Steve1 said, "Good morning", while I was washing my hands outside the mess tent.

I replied, "Don't talk to me, you're two-faced and you expect me to be okay with you when you talk about me behind my back!"

Other people heard this and he walked away with his head down. He was quiet during breakfast and I felt better for telling him how much he had upset me.

We set off up the rugged, steep, shale and rocky mountain. It was very hard-going through fierce gale-force winds, snow and rain, making visibility poor. It was also dangerously slippy underfoot. Then the hailstones came as we got higher, then more blizzards of freezing snow as we reached 4600m. We were fighting against the elements and my head was aching. I was told to drink four litres of water every day, but conditions made it hard to.

"Pole! Pole!" African guides said as they passed us. It means "slowly, slowly," in their language (Swahili).

They said it so I would have a better chance of getting to the top and of staying well.

Also they said, "Jambo," which means "hello, how are you?"

"Mazoora," I replied, which means, "I am well".

This broke the day up for me and made me feel happy. They were happy too, that I spoke a little of their language and smiled and nodded back to me.

We reached the top of LAVA ROCK. This had been the toughest, most tiring climb so far. Steve1 came over to say well done and sorry for how he had treated me. I was already feeling overwhelmed with emotion at accomplishing the challenging climb and was crying to myself. He caught me off guard.

I just said, "I should think so."

We had lunch in the heavy snow under a plastic elasticated cover Matt had brought. All of us huddled together trying to eat our sandwiches, chicken leg, fruit, cake and a carton of juice whilst trying to keep warm and dry.

After lunch we climbed across from the snowy side of the mountain down onto the tropical side, where there were more black, sharp and very jagged rocks. The landscape was harsh but at the same time pretty

Gruelling eight hour climb to lava tower and then back down the tropical side, the mountain ever changing.

The Lava Tower

The Tropical Side

because it was softened by the palm trees, plants, tropical flowers, streams and waterfalls. As suspected, it was indeed hard work ascending and descending and when the camp came into view, it was a welcome sight and I couldn't wait to rest.

Its 6.10pm and dinner is at 6.30pm. My head is banging all the time now, even tablets aren't working and I tried to nap at 5.30pm today but can't sleep again! Don't know how much longer I can keep my mind and body running without sleep. The camp is once again full of chatter.

The day was full of wonderful sights as the mountain is forever changing and the spirit of the cheerful guides keeps everyone going. Our porters are a great help carrying our bags to the next camp but still my back is nearly giving way. My rucksack weighs about 6kg and despite using my poles (which isn't always possible) to help take the weight off my lower body, I am going through painkillers like no-tomorrow. I'd packed my ukulele hoping we'd have camp fires on an evening, but government laws forbid this because of the stripping of the forest and the damage and mess it would cause. Consequently there is never any real warmth to the camps. Everyone is concentrating on working hard to conquer Kilimanjaro and as long as I conquer my mountain, that's okay. It rained most of the three hours coming down the tropical side today, but nevertheless it was a lot warmer. Sometimes I prefer the hailstones, it's dryer somehow. Luckily, I had my umbrella and nobody else has one in our group. The guide, Nelson, calls me Umbrella Girl and smart for having one like him! It's been a god-send. He gets us all singing "Jambo Jambo Bwana, Habarigana, Zuri Suna Zuri Sune, Wageni Mwakaribishwa,Kilimanjaro,Hakunamatata," making lots of fun for us to keep our spirits up.

It's 6.25pm now, so off to the loo and wash before tea.

PLEASE GOD HELP ME SLEEP TONIGHT.

Day 8

21st Feb 2014

Karanga camp – 4650m/15,090ft

Its 5.30am, time to get up for our next climb to camp five. This is going to be a five hour uphill climb and will be rocky and dangerous. We will be encountering

Barranco Wall, which is apparently very steep. When we reach camp we will have lunch at 1pm and then we will be able to rest. Whoop Whoop! I asked Matt for a Diamox last night, a prescription drug to help with altitude sickness. He said I could have half a tablet and I took two painkillers and guess what? I slept most of the night and dreamt about flying black seals and the church.

I feel much rested compared to other mornings. Today we will climb to 4033m. Kilimanjaro's snowy summit is right outside my tent now, so near, yet I still have two days to go before reaching the crater on summit day.

I'm home-sick because I still can't make any phone calls. When I reach the hotel after the climb I will call my children. I feel a little anxious, as I do every morning. Even being here doesn't take that life-long feeling of insecurity away. It is dark and I am wearing my head torch as usual and I have to pack up my things before breakfast. Everyone is chatting and doing the same. I am finding this trip a lot harder than I first thought it would be. I haven't washed my hair or seen my whole body since I set off. I am using wet wipes for a combat wash in my tent as we don't have much privacy and I use a small bowl of water they give you at the end of your day's climb to wash my face and feet in. My sleeping sack and liner are always wet with condensation in the morning as I pack up and my fingers have pins and needles from the cold. They hurt as I try to stuff my sleeping sack into its sleeve and my feet are hurting the same.

I set off at 7am, determined to make the difficult climb up the face of the mountain. We climbed on dangerous rocks, balancing on the edge of the shelf with sheer drops below. They call this the Barranco Wall. I had to cling on for dear life and haul myself up the rock face. It was extremely steep and rocky and if you were to put a foot wrong, you'd be dead. I lead most of the time with Reg or Thomas. They said I was good and as strong as the guys. Steve1 and Matt said how impressed they were with my climbing skills. We then climbed down into a valley and ascended back up again to camp. The small rivers we crossed and the waterfalls were again so pretty but the sparse vegetation and giant volcanic rocks and shale made it look very barren.

It is 4pm and I've just woken up from a siesta having arrived in camp at 12 noon. I am relieved it has only been a five hour climb today. I was happy we had home-

made chicken and chips, vegetables and cucumber with tomato ketchup for lunch - a touch of home. I always drink lots of tea and water to hydrate me. If I don't, I get head-achey because the fluids produce more red blood cells, helping to prevent altitude sickness. It's thundering and raining again, as it does most days after 1pm. Tomorrow we go to Barafu camp at 4673m; this will be our last camp before we set off at midnight on the final eighteen hour climb. Even though I have napped this afternoon, I am still tired, so hope I sleep after dinner. I need all my strength to complete the expedition. I smile with tears in my eyes at saying this, "I'm daft!"

Ciaran, an Irish man, let me use his phone to call Ella and Jake today. It was the first time in eight days and it was emotional hearing Ella's voice. I wanted to pull her through the phone to cuddle and kiss her beautiful face. She reassured me she is okay at home and I'm happier now I have talked with her. As we blew kisses down the phone I cried with joy, "get a grip Carol!"

Jake wasn't there, sadly. Still, one phone call and one text is what Ciaran said I could have, so I sent a text to Stuart and was happy to receive one back. Both of them gave me encouragement and loving wishes.

I like sharing with Celine, we get on and she doesn't get up at 5am to organise her things like Ying Ying. I asked her if she wanted a cup-a-tea.

She asked, in her comical Chinese accent, "what is a cup-a-tea?"

I describe with my hands a cup and with the other hand I poured tea.

She said, "Haaaaaaa cup of tea! You talk very fast."

In a way Steve1 did me a favour by causing me and Ying Ying to fall out, because she drove me mad with all her belongings! Still, she had given me a small travel towel at the beginning of the trip which has been a god-send. Celine gave me three travel Johns that I pee into inside my tent at night because it's too cold to get up and go outside. This is a very intricate manoeuvre with all your clothes on. They are brilliant because I have to drink so much to stop me getting sick. My pee crystallises into a solid block, so when

I'm done and the bag's full, I put it in the doorway outside my tent. Just done one now, so thought I'd share it with you before I turn my light out and go to sleep.

Dinner is in half an hour; I'm not hungry but will force myself to eat, if I have to, to keep my energy level up. Steve1 did not eat a lot at dinner last night and this afternoon he sleeps without food again, no wonder he says he feels like crap. I am beginning to see that climbing this mountain is a game of strategy and playing it isn't easy.

This evening will be the last full night's sleep before we head for the summit tomorrow evening. I have felt the great rock beneath me for several days and sensed her vastness. However, it is not possible to see all of her, she is far too big. The mountains I've seen previously look like peanuts in comparison to the great Mount Kilimanjaro. She is a beauty and I have much respect for what the volcanic eruptions have created. My breathing is short and shallow and I have to move about slowly to conserve energy and regulate my breathing. I pray she will help me conquer her tomorrow and the next day. I feel like I have made a friend forever

Close to reaching my dream at the top of the world.

and I will never forget her.

Good Night x.

Day 9

22ⁿᵈ Feb 2014

Barafu camp – 4640m/15,223ft

We woke at 5.30am and set off from camp six at 7.15am heading for Barafu. We trekked across vast plains of ash, shale and huge rocks. The walking seemed never-ending but eventually we stopped at 11.30am. It was one of the rare times the sun had really shone on us this trip. Both Steves' faces were all chapped and scabby from exposure to the elements. Thank goodness I wore sunscreen! There are so many giant rocks and our tents looked funny squeezed in between them, perched at the edge of the mountain, looking down onto the plateau. The mountain is dotted with different coloured tents and bags and alive with chatter.

It requires about fifteen porters as well as the guides to make this trip possible. They carry water from the rivers, boiling it to prevent us from getting ill. Other tasks they carry out are cooking, keeping the loo clean, and carrying our tents, kitchen equipment, picnic table and chairs all on their backs and heads. The rivers are sparse now at this high altitude so we have to be careful to conserve the water we have. There is not enough time to cool it and it is boiling hot in our bottle, making it hard to drink.

I complain to Matt, who says, "stop putting it in bed with you to keep you warm, then it will get cold."

I tell him: "I can't help it, its freezing at night even with all my layers on." Living on this harsh mountain is like nothing I have ever experienced in my life.

The porters and guides were fit and strong and continued to keep us motivated by singing songs. They are very poor and have to rely on tips from climbers at the end of each trip. They never have the opportunity to leave their country. They chatted in Swahili to each other although some of them spoke a little English, usually only the guides. There was Charles, who I called King Charles the 1st.There was Nelson and I would say to him, "hey, Nelson Mandela has returned." He was a young, handsome, clever man! There was Thomas, who had a sound, gentlemanly, serious look about him and he was their leader. Reg, who I called Captain Reginald, had a great smile! They were all friendly African men who always said, "Hakuna Matata," which means, "no worries for the rest of your days." They really were cool guys, forever helpful and encouraging.

We arrived in Camp Seven soon after midday and had our lunch. Matt told us to sleep until tea time but I found this virtually impossible with all the other climbers walking noisily past my tent. The evening meal was at 5pm, after which we were advised to sleep again until 10.30pm in order that we rested before we started our climb at midnight. At dinner we were briefed on what to wear and what to take in our rucksack. Mine would be heavy!

I borrowed most of my army gear from my friends Darren and Denise who have been on many adventures and I felt sure I had the right clothes for the freezing conditions. Some of his padded trousers, in particular, along with his wife's Long-Johns, kept me warm and helped to cushion me when sleeping on the hard, cold rock at night. His buffalo coat was invaluable, as I slept in it most nights. I still had to pay for a lot of my own gear myself, including climbing boots. There was also the visa to pay for and the tips at the end of the climb. The list was endless and I was skint.

Thankfully my new Italian friend Antonio, who I'd met at his restaurant, Rustico's, was interested in my story. He had just lost his mum to cancer and much to my surprise, generously gave me a gift of £600 towards my trip. Thanks to this, I had all the right equipment and felt comfortable and quite confident I'd packed everything I needed and would be warm enough.

Celine is trying on her layers next to me. She flew from China with Lisa who is also a friend of Ying Ying. Between them they have an African porter, Frank, who carries their extra layers, poles, sunglasses, creams, cameras and energy bars. For the entire trip they haven't carried anything except their water and I am the only lady here who carries her own gear, like the men. I will have muscles like Popeye! My back is hurting so much now that I have to be careful bending down and my legs and knees are becoming weaker from the weight and climb. My bowel and hernia are troubling me a lot but I am determined I will make it, even though Matt tells us we will feel like crap. He says we will hardly be able to breathe, have banging headaches and will stagger drunkenly. We may hallucinate and we will suffer from sickness and tiredness, all as a result of the altitude. He has got a special tent in case anyone gets seriously ill. It's a bit like a decompression chamber, which in emergencies you can pump oxygen into. For less serious situations, he has a case of other medication and oxygen.

Imagine being this high up above the

clouds, we are as high as the planes fly. The sky has been our home for the last few days and soon I will see into the heart of Kilimanjaro. From Barafu camp we will be climbing to a height of 6000m, that's the equivalent of climbing twelve football pitches on top of each other. I am a little worried I will not be well enough to make it. The ascent to Lava Tower was the equivalent of about seven pitches on top of each other and until now that's the most we have climbed in one day.

After hearing Steve1 offer to carry Ying Ying's water tonight, I couldn't help feeling disappointed that I have had no support from him. I have, after all, been doing this climb to raise money for his charity.

I'm tired now, so hope I sleep the four and a half hours, otherwise I'll be knackered. Even though I am looking forward to conquering this giant, volcanic mountain, I'm glad this is our second to last night. If I see another bowl of soup and maize I'll be sick, I swear! It's so hard getting comfy on the cold rocks and packing and unpacking everyday on time is a rush. I've had enough.

We were woken at 10.30pm, not that I'd

One of the rare days the Sun shone on us.

The sky was my home for eight days.

had much sleep because sleeping and eating on demand at this altitude is hard. Tonight is the big finale. How can you be expected to sleep, with the excited buzz from the entire camp, the sense of anticipation and the feeling of apprehension about whether we will reach the summit?

Day 10

23rd Feb 2014

Summit Night! 4640m/15,223ft

We set off at midnight towards the Uhuru Peak, the summit. We had an eighteen hour journey ahead. Even though the sky was clear and full of stars with a beautiful red, crescent moon, we needed our head torches to light the way. After all the rain we'd had, it was a perfect evening. I was surprised at how steep it was, practically vertical but I kept my head down, concentrating on navigating the dangerous climb, working my way slowly upwards. I looked up and it seemed like I was climbing the stairway to heaven. When I glanced down, my heart was in my mouth and my stomach lunged. I was scared of the expanse between me and what lay below and I dare not look down again.

I stood beneath the vast mountain, thinking, *just me and you now!*

We kept stopping each hour for four minute breaks and this was doing my head in because my fingers and toes got cold straight away. Some of our group were flagging after about two hours. During the rests I would stop for a drink and eat an energy sweet which Matt had given me. The gradient was still extremely steep but I had been given so many tips back home on how to conquer her, I knew I must keep going. My mp4 player played only four songs before it ran out of charge, I was gutted. Still, it played, "Inupendi with no worries on your mind; it just takes two to make it through…." This song kept me going. Also, I was watching Thomas's rest-stepping and breathing techniques. I had already learnt to do the breathing and it helped a lot to watch him climb. He had a massive rucksack that weighed a ton on his back and he was almost bent in two. In fact, Celine panicked and asked what was up with Thomas, as he walked bent and slow.

We had five guides with us and eight climbers, the porters remained back at the last camp. Some in the group were flagging and I was frightened when I saw Steve2 begin to stagger towards the edge of the mountain. I was frantically shouting for others to grab him but nobody heard, so I ran back down. The ground was rocky, thick with snow and underlying ice. I went to grab him and thought that if I wasn't careful, he could take me with him. I managed to pull him back, just as he reached the edge of the dangerous, snowy shelf. All around me others were throwing up, some more than just once. After three or four hours they were getting too tired to carry on. I knew I couldn't stop again but some people wanted more breaks. I got into a good rhythm, unlike others who were wearing themselves out. I was using my poles a lot by then but not stopping, just pacing and breathing in deeply and slowly letting all my breath out from in between pursed lips. Everyone wanted to keep stopping.

I was saying, "No, I'll get cold. I have to keep going."

I felt like they were holding me back.

After four hours in the pitch black, Wise Thomas, the leader, called King Charles to the front of the group where I was.

He said, "Take this girl up this mountain now."

It was like music to my ears and the two of us set off at a slow but rhythmic pace. I was happy I had left the group behind.

I was going at a steady pace but feeling so tired that I was hallucinating. I just wanted to close my eyes and roll over in the snow which appeared to be like a big, white, cuddly duvet. I wanted to stop and rest, but I

Magnificent red sunrise after climbing in the dark for 7 hours was a welcome sight.

I thought I was at the top but still had further to go.

knew if I did, I wouldn't get started again. I kept sucking on energy sweets but eventually couldn't eat anymore. My mind and body needed a push as I fought to keep my eyes open. I thought of Jake, Ella and Leanne (my son's fiancée).

In my mind they were shouting, "Go on Mum you can do it!"

Jake was saying, "Look at her! She's half hour in front of the others, go on Mum! Go on you can do it!"

Ella was pushing me on, too, so I really believe that they were the ones that got me up my mountain.

The sun was starting to rise, lighting up the whole sky, which was bright red. It looked amazing and I could now see the Africa which, until now, had only been visible from the night lights shining from the distant towns and villages. I stopped to take a picture of its breath-taking beauty. Charles took one of me, for which I am forever grateful, as I love that photo and it takes pride of place on my mantelpiece.

We reached Stella Point as the sun continued to rise and took more pictures. I thought we were at the summit, but Charles told me we weren't. I was disappointed because I was exhausted but still happy I had made it this far. As we climbed on I was surprised to see other fit climbers being marched speedily down the mountain, some were not able to stand up straight due to altitude sickness.

The final frill on the cake: looked like icing drizzling down it.

My promised kept for the amazingly talented Dr Fawole, I love him (name spelling might be different, emotions still the same!)

It made me think I had better take it slow; don't rush this last bit. Pole! Pole!

I kept pushing slowly upwards until I could see the great glacier stretching across the mountain's edge, like a decorative frill on a cake. The views were out of this world. It was unlike anything I had seen before.

We were approaching the crater's edge and I was soon looking into the heart of my mountain. The chasm was not as deep as I had expected and as I looked down into it, I could imagine how it had once erupted and envisaged the heat rising and the scorching, liquid lava, thrusting towards the heavens. I could appreciate its great power, both to create beauty and destroy it!

Uhuru Peak – 6000m/20,000ft

We reached UHURU PEAK at 7.30am, seven and a half hours after setting off. I made it with King Charles! I WAS AT THE VERY TOP. We hugged and congratulated each other on our success. Once again, I cried to myself with joy and sang songs with Charles. I felt a great sense of freedom and relief, especially as I had been unsure whether I would die from cancer and now from the effects of altitude. I asked other climbers to take pictures of me and Charles at the summit. I wrote in the snow with my pole DR FAWOLE + CAROL and took a photo. Dr Fawole, was my surgeon, who had saved my life by removing my bowel cancer eight months earlier.

He said, "I have stood at the bottom of Mount

Kilimanjaro but there is no way I am going up it."

He laughed and promised he would make me fit enough to fulfil my dream, on condition I took his name and left it at the summit.

We did it! We kept our promises.

"PEACE TO THE WORLD, I AM A CHAMPION," I shouted, jumping up and down, on top of the world!

It might have been the loneliest, quietest part of the world, but even so, I was buzzing. I had done it and nobody else from our group was there yet. I realised I was first up, despite all my surgery and even after I had been out of training for a few weeks whilst I healed and fund-raised. I was shocked and amazed at my own achievement!

After only fifteen minutes at the top, it was starting to get cold and after more pictures we had to leave, as we were literally starting to freeze. Charles gave me water with pain killers because he could see I was suffering and my whole body and head was hurting. I could see other climbers slowly struggling to make their way to the summit, feeling the pressure of not having much air to breathe.

We made our way back down to Stella Point, passing our group en-route. We sat and had a cup of tea and an energy bar, enjoying the breath-taking views. Strangers from all nationalities gathered there, some

Peace to the world, I am a champion! I shouted with exhilaration and fulfillment, stood at the summit of Kilimanjaro with King Charles.

smiling and chattering about what they had accomplished, sadly others were struggling to go any further and some never did make it all the way, *bless 'em*. It was a bright sunny day and I took two layers off and put my shades on before we began the descent down a different route to camp Barafu.

I was surprised to see all the thick soil, rocks, shale and ash we had to walk through as we descended. There was just me and Charles so we were able to set off at speed, sliding down the mountain. I used my poles like I was skiing on snow, around and over rocks, dodging people coming down, I was flying past them.

"WOOO WOOO."

It was great fun. Charles was shaking his head, laughing at me.

He said, "I ain't ever seen a lady as strong as you in my life."

Barafu camp – 4640m/15,223ft

We got down the mountain in a record time of two hours. By 10am I was back in camp and the porters made me a cup of tea. I put my feet up in the blazing sunshine, waiting for the others to return. The porters said how strong I was and laughed at me as Charles filled them in on our adventure. They were impressed

...aid I should get a degree in climbing!

It's been a tough challenge, camping and climbing with strangers. I had not anticipated just how hard it would be and although I have loved it, I wish I had company. Everyone already knew someone else on the climb except me, James and Ciaran and it got quite lonely at times, especially as I couldn't easily contact home.

Others were coming into base now, James first, followed by Ciaran and Matt. We congratulated each other.

Later, I was resting in my tent when I heard Steve1 say to Matt, "Wasn't Carol superb?"

I wish he'd said it to me.

Hours later, the rest drifted into camp. The Chinese ladies were at the back, not arriving until after 1pm. something had freaked them out, although I don't know what and Matt had to go back up and bring them down. I heard that Steve1 was last up to the summit and had really suffered from altitude sickness, which made him struggle to get his breath. He was stumbling all over while Nelson held and pushed him up the mountain.

Steve1 was saying to him, "I'm going to die, Nelson."

In a way I am glad he found it tough! On one

occasion back home at the gym, he had confidently said that he believed whether you get altitude sickness or not depends on your strength of mind. Whereas I had been told it is like sea sickness: you either have it, or you don't. Who knows?

We have just eaten and I'm in my tent waiting for the others to rest. After this we will set off to Millenium Camp, for our last night on the mountain. Tomorrow we have a tough five hour steep trek through more jungle and rocky terrain. Then the Land Rovers will pick us up for the drive to the final gates and then to the Keys Hotel. Celine tells me it's not a great hotel, but I'm looking forward to a shower and bed.

Millenium Camp – 3837m/12,590ft

I have arrived in camp now and it rained for hours on the descent. It is nearly dinner time, 7pm. I can't bear more soup and vegetables. I feel sick at the thought of it. The meat ran out a couple of days ago.

After dinner in the mess tent, we calculated what we should pay in tips to the cooks, toilet man, guides and porters. We have decided between the eight of us to give $205each.

I've had less than four hours sleep in the

last day and a half and we have to wake at 5am again! AHHHRG!

Now most of my challenge is complete, it seems like I've been living in a dream, in fact surreal best describes how I feel. I am extremely emotional with joy at having made it. I am also extremely knackered and can't wait for my own bed when I get home.

Goodnight World, I've been to the top of you today.

Day 11

24th Feb 2014

I woke at 4.30am and packed up for the last time. We were due to leave at 5.30am, after breakfast. During breakfast Matt told me the Chinese ladies were going to be picked up by the mountain rescue Land Rover and taken to the gates, as they couldn't walk any further. I asked him if I could go too and he said I could, if I was sick. I told him my hernia was killing me so he agreed. I was back in my tent and suddenly realised that if I took the lift for the final part of the journey, I wouldn't have fully completed my challenge. I took more pain killers and told Matt I didn't want the lift after all.

It was a hard, steep, six hour descent, longer than expected. My knees and elbows were especially hurting and the rest of my body shook with pain when my feet touched the ground, due to the steepness. On previous days, I had been in front throughout, but now I was near the rear with Charles at my side. The Chinese ladies were at the back taking it easy, waiting for their lift. Every step I took felt like hell and I wanted the gates to come into sight to rescue me.

We stopped for a rest before we reached the gates. Reg looked at me and must have thought, *that poor girl*.

He asked, "Can I carry your rucksack?"

"Yes." I said, gladly.

When I saw him struggling with his own as well as mine, though, I asked him to give it back but he wouldn't and insisted on carrying it. Finally we reached the flat ground and I was so relieved that I cried again to myself.

As I hobbled through the gates I felt a real sense of achievement and wanted a beer to celebrate the fact I had MADE MY DREAM COME TRUE! I was asked to take shelter, from the beating sun, with the others. Some were having their boots shined.

I felt restless, feeling I was missing an opportunity and got up, looking for my mate King Charles. I bumped into Matt, who asked me if I wanted a drink and where I was going. I went with him to the bar, which was just an old wooden hut. He handed me an African beer, my first in eleven days and we congratulated each other.

I found Charles and he took me to meet his friends, who were selling souvenirs. I sat and haggled with them for presents to take home.

I loved Charles and his friends, they seemed carefree and friendly. The other climbers never moved from where they had been asked to sit, missing the chance to buy gifts or experience the culture. I was pleased with what I had bought: a T shirt with a map of the mountain on it, a carved salad serving set, a beautifully painted canvas of my mountain with a giraffe and elephants on it, and amazing jewellery.

Matt then came to hurry me, as the tip ceremony was about to begin. I ran back to the others, who were all waiting. Each member of the group had tips to give and I was handed two envelopes with dollars in for Reg and Thomas. The porters and guides sang and danced for us as we clapped and savoured this moving moment, knowing it was coming to an end. James then gave a touching speech about how we had all come on this journey for our own different reasons. This brought a lump to my throat. As their names were called one by one, we gave out the tips and everyone thanked them and shook hands or hugged. Again, a very moving scene.

A driver called Charles (who had originally brought us here and who drove like a rally driver) picked us up and we drove to the Keys Hotel, passing villages, coffee plantations, banana trees, shops and more.

During the drive, I heard Steve1 say that there was nothing much to report home. All he had seen in Africa was jungle, where animal life had been poached and poor running boys who fetched and carried up the mountain for foreign climbers.

This is not at all how I would describe my experience of Africa.

The animals tend to shy away from humans and the jungle is huge. Nevertheless, I had seen different species of monkeys and birds. Nelson reassured me that there are plenty of animals because poaching is not allowed in Tanzania. If a poacher is caught killing animals, the law allows the poacher to be killed. As for the porters and guides, they seem happy in their work, which keeps them fit and strong and earns them a living. They are very proud and I admire them greatly for their strength of character and courage. It is not an easy job and every year the mountain takes lives.

We arrived at the Keys Hotel and I took the shower I had been longing for. I saw all of my body for the first time since arriving in Africa. My room was basic but a palace in comparison to the two man tent I had been living in.

I enjoyed changing out of my climbing gear into my short summer dress. When I met Lisa, Celine and Ying Ying as I came out of my room, they laughed and said they didn't recognise me with my legs out.

It felt good.

We were buzzing and ready to go down to the restaurant for pizza and coke with all the others. After we had eaten Matt and the guides gave out certificates for successfully reaching the summit. Yet another emotional moment as we celebrated and congratulated each other. The time came for everyone to say their goodbyes and leave for the airport. Not me, though, because I had another adventure ahead.

I am now lying by the pool sun bathing, enjoying a Malibu and pineapple, surrounded by palm trees blowing in the breeze. Naomi and Ibelieve, who are local African girls, stop to say hello, as do some of the local men, who are friendly and chatty too. The girls say I am cute! I am resting my body and my mind, giving myself a chance to recover. As I begin to

The tip-giving ceremony. James said we had all come for our own different reasons, bringing a lump to my throat.

Receiving my certificate, a very proud moment.

reflect, I think back to when it all started and to what I have achieved and experienced in the last year! Tomorrow I will be picked up at 8am to start my safari.

PART 2

Making The Dream Come True

I had been looking at The Great Mount Kilimanjaro, in Tanzania, in my book, *The Land, Extreme Earth*. I was in awe of the biggest free-standing mountain on Earth. It stands at 20,000ft, four miles up into the sky. A universal force or energy was drawing me towards it.

One morning at the gym where I'm a member, I was asked if I wanted to join in a 'spinnathon' to help raise money to set up a local charity called The Laila Milly Foundation. Its aim was to create a day respite centre for mums and dads, families and carers of handicapped babies and children up to five years old who had been born with life threatening illnesses. I thought this was a great idea as I knew from first-hand experience what it was like to look after someone with special needs.

*

My sister, Donna, was born with brain damage and Grand-mal epilepsy which could not be controlled. She was on the highest dosage of medication I have ever known a child to take. She took a total of seventeen tablets a day, including Epilim, Tegratol and Mogadon, all crushed between two spoons until she was old enough to swallow them whole. Hence I took care of her most of the time and we were almost joined at the hip.

Donna and I shared a bed, so if she had a fit in the night I could hold her to prevent her falling out, as she had done many times. Donna was one year older than me and was very strong and heavy. Her screaming would increase into a crescendo of murderous roars, full of fear, each time making me jump and making my heart pound. Her blue pursed lips and wide green eyes showed she was scared for her life and was trying to stop herself from going into the Big Black Hole, as she later described it to me! She would come round after a few minutes, exhausted and drip white. Fits could last up to half an hour and many times the doctor would come to our house and sedate Donna and when this didn't work, he would call an ambulance to take her to hospital. Sometimes her temperature would soar through the roof, causing her seizures to run into one another and become out of control. They would often last for days.

Donna once had a stroke, brought on by falling during a seizure: she had smashed her head on the corner of the stone fireplace in our front room. She was so strong she even recovered from that. Many a time, when I heard that first cry, I would run and slide underneath her on my knees to catch her head to prevent it from bouncing off the floor. I knew her lifeless body would rapidly drop, collapsing like a sack-o-taties, causing serious injury. She would pull at her clothes, try to take her pants off, all the while thrashing about, struggling with jerky movements. She had no concept that I was there, trying to preserve her dignity and stop her from hurting herself. It wasn't until she started to come out of the seizure that Donna realised I was with her.

I comforted her, saying 'I'm here Donna, you're okay'. I stroked her forehead and face, gently tapping her cheeks, talking her back to normality, holding her firmly close to me. She lay flopped out with her head on my legs, trying to regain her energy and bearings, just wanting to fall asleep.

We went everywhere together. After Donna got home from her special needs school (Lidgate, NewMill, Holmfirth) and when I'd finished helping mum with the housework or helping dad to tend the land, which we rented from farmers, we would go playing in the woods and pick bluebells for mum. Or we would go to the swings on our bikes, riding over the fields, hills and by streams where we grew up. Even though she fitted and fell off a lot, I was determined Donna would enjoy the same in life as me whenever she could.

When I was eleven and Donna twelve, I was told to take her to the swimming baths in the next village. We had to walk two miles to get there. It was in the six weeks school holiday and the pool was full of screaming kids enjoying themselves. Unbeknownst to me she had a fit, no doubt triggered by excitement. I couldn't hear her scream like I normally would but my instincts told me to turn round.

Donna was on the pool floor, at my feet.

I screamed for help and an attendant pulled her out of the water. I remember thinking, *how long has she been there?* She wasn't breathing and I was petrified, standing there thinking my sister was dying. The attendant gave her mouth-to-mouth resuscitation and she came round and was rushed to hospital by ambulance.

I walked home and got a hiding for taking my eyes off my sister.

Nevertheless, I understood how hard it was for all of us living with Donna's illness. It was such a great responsibility. When Donna was a young teenager my mum couldn't cope with her disability combined with the extreme abusive environment in which we all lived. If there had been a respite centre, I am sure Donna would have gone there. Instead, she was put into care with children with behaviour problems, where she was bullied and abused by some of the kids. It broke my heart to see her there.

*

I took up the spinning challenge and found myself

in a class of people with twenty bikes in. I was having fun peddling to music and playing games for an hour with Maya, the lady whose charity it was. I didn't know then that Maya was Laila Milly's mum.

Laila Milly had been born with a rare neurological condition called Aicardi Syndrome. Laila's syndrome meant she had an enlarged heart, the central part of her brain was absent and she had lesions on her eyes, a curved spine and epilepsy that couldn't be controlled.

Sadly, Laila passed away on the 2nd of March, a day before her first birthday. She had been a brave little girl, who had inspired her parents to do something positive in her memory by setting up a charity. I was reminded of how brave Donna had been, living with her disability. Even though her illness wasn't as severe as Laila's, Donna still needed 24/7 care and there had only been my mum and I to give it most of the time.

My family experience gave me the determination to raise money to help other suffering parents and siblings who have no respite support. This is why it was so close to my heart.

I had enjoyed taking a sponsor sheet around my street, telling friends and neighbours about the charity. I explained that The Laila Milly building was fitted out with a sensory vision room and other rooms suitable for activities to aid the children's development. It also had a wheelchair friendly lift. It was beginning to look like a care centre and was nearly ready for opening in the spring. However, ongoing funds were needed to keep it open in the future, in order to pay nurses and overheads. This is why they needed people to get involved and to raise sponsorship and awareness. I raised one hundred and fifty pounds in such a short time for this great cause and was amazed at everyone's kindness and generosity.

The next challenge, planned by Steve1 and Maya, was to climb Mount Kilimanjaro. They were looking for volunteers and had all the information in a booklet which they left on the counter at my gym. I asked if anyone else was interested because I was thinking about taking one. I already knew that I was going to do it! It was my type of challenge! And I had more than one good reason to want to climb this mountain. That decided it for me!

My curiosity had been aroused and I was interested in finding out what it would entail to climb Kilimanjaro. I am an adrenalin junkie and have jumped out of a plane twice with the Red Devils at 13,500ft and this mountain was going to be 20,000ft. This got me wondering what the sky would be like as my home for ten days and whether breathing up there would be possible. I have my scuba diver rescue certificate and have dived to 50m, seeing the abyss and mountains under the sea. I have skied across country and down many mountains in various countries around the world.

I have climbed a few mountains in England and Wales, small in comparison and loved painting them. Nothing like Kilimanjaro, though. My vision of the Earth's expanse was becoming bigger and my passion for seeing mountains and their stunning views and locations was increasing.

The Laila Milly Foundation wanted at least twelve people to take on the climb and a few started showing an interest. For those interested, they had arranged a presentation at the fire station where Steve1 worked, given by the Jagged Globe Company, who would be organizing the expedition. Avid climbers and walkers attended and we were shown a map of the route we would be taking, highlighting how tough the climb of Kilimanjaro would be. They talked about the equipment and provisions needed and advised us that we would have to raise £3,500 in order to take part. With less than a year to go and much to do, *would it be possible*?

In my mind and heart I wanted to take up this challenge but I didn't know if my body could do it. I had three different operations in my lower abdomen, the most recent of which was my hernia operation only 3 months before. This was still causing me problems. Despite this element of doubt, I was determined to attempt this dream challenge.

*

I was not an avid climber, my biggest mountain so far had been Scafell Pike in the Lake District and that had been tough. I knew for sure I would have to vastly improve my fitness level. During the latest operation my surgeon had made his insertion through my old caesarean scar. He was supposed to repair a femoral hernia. However, he took it upon himself to repair my inguinal one as well, even though there was nothing wrong with it. I had woken up in so much pain I had to be given morphine. The nurses were lovely but my surgeon came to me laughing when I was in recovery, saying he had diagnosed the wrong one and said he'd repaired them both.

I asked him, "Why?"

He replied, "Just in case the other one goes."

"Was there something wrong with the other one?"

"No," he answered, "And there won't be now".

He told the nurse to send me home, much to both our surprise. She was obviously doubtful because she double-checked with the sister whether I ought to be discharged to the care of my fourteen year old daughter.

She returned saying, "No way."

The surgeon said, "She can use a phone." This meant if anything were to go wrong, my daughter could ring the hospital.

I was shaking and crying, I think my body was in shock. They gave me tea and biscuits because the morphine was making me dizzy and sick.

I was concerned at the thought of Ella seeing me like that, as it would have traumatized her for life and put her off having any surgery in future herself.

I hated what the surgeon did to me because I knew there were too many foreign bodies inside me. There was so much meshing on my slim frame, that it was restricting my movement. I could feel it through my skin and it was causing lumps and creating painful scar tissue, which resulted in nerve damage. Hot pain would shoot down my leg from my groin.

My friend came to pick me up from the hospital the next morning after I rang her. It took Catherine and the staff over two hours to find me as there was no record of me. I hadn't even been booked onto the ward after coming out of theatre. Catherine wheeled me out to the car and away from what felt like a horror story.

The poor practice was further highlighted when the nurse came to take out my eight clips ten days later at home. She could not remove them because they were too tight. She said she had never seen anything like it in her career and would have to come back with a different pair of staple cutters the next day. I was in a lot of pain so when she arrived the next morning I was already sweating and shaking. She tried again to put the cutters under the metal staples but the blades were too thick for them. She said I would have to go into hospital to have them removed but I pleaded with her to let me have a go with the cutters because I did not want to return to the hospital.

I knew my own pain threshold.

I pushed down, digging into my skin until I cut the metal clips and the nurse eased them out with tweezers, making my skin bleed. I am still living with the specialist's mistakes. The upside of this, is that my friends brought me buns and flowers, they gave me help and support and we had lots of laughs in the process.

A couple of weeks later my friend Paula picked me up to take me to the pool at my gym for the first time. I continued to visit the pool and would walk up and down in the water pulling myself along with my arms. I hated being weak and could no longer use weights like I had all my life. I always need to feel strong and this was another time when I knew I had to pull through to cope with the needs and demands of my teenagers.

*

Not long after the Jagged Globe presentation, I made a final decision to go for it, to climb Mount Kilimanjaro.

Despite my recent operation, I decided to start bag-packing in the supermarkets, along with my children and Maya, in order to raise funds.

I asked more and more people to sponsor this great cause, and they did. This gave me hope and determination to carry on. When I told friends and strangers about the charity everyone wanted to give, and this gave me faith to continue. As long as I could keep coming up with new ideas to raise funds, there would be no problem reaching the target of £3,500.

I have been modelling for a few years and I had this idea that my photographer Leo and I could put on an exhibition of his images of beautiful nude women. I decided it would be at the Frog n Moose pub in Ackworth and Dean, the owner, kindly offered the room and bar staff for free.

Leo is a friend and great inspiration to me. He had published two books, the first called *Why Nude?* and the second called *Sublime Nude.* I feature in both books. His work depicts images of beautiful women in exquisite poses in numerous and contrasting locations. It demonstrates the sublime beauty and innocence of humans, which he believes only God can create and it shows the emotions and struggles with life most of us inevitably experience.

Leo was wonderfully generous and excited to go with my idea as he always wanted to exhibit his amazing photography of the nude models he so passionately captured.

Leo had a boxful of beautifully printed posters of a nude lady posing as the statue of liberty. We distributed them to a few art galleries in Yorkshire, colleges, shops and libraries. You name it, we posted them everywhere, even on Facebook and advertised in the local paper.

It took six months to organize all the exhibition prints as they cost Leo a lot of money and took time to be professionally mounted. They were to be placed onto beautiful ruby red table clothes, lit by chandeliers to accentuate the beauty of the models. A lady artist, Carol, was there with her painted versions of his work. Other models from his two books also came to the event. Leo gave a talk and slide show about all his work and I gave a very nervous presentation about why I was doing this.

Thirty people came throughout the day and thoroughly enjoyed the exhibition, showing genuine interest in Leo's work and my fundraising efforts. There was a quiz, raffle and a bar. The soft music we provided created a great ambience. I believed it was going to be a great success and would raise lots of interest and money. Although it turned out to be a lovely day, I was disappointed at the amount of people who attended and in the end we only raised £150. It had cost Leo hundreds to facilitate.

Capturing my innocence and building my confidence.

This picture is taken from Leo Rosser's book entitled "Why Nude".

It was going to be a lot harder than I first thought!

I was having to contend with the pain from my hernia operation, deal with work and home life, all the time trying to improve my fitness whilst still finding time to fundraise. Added to this, I was starting to discover that there was a lot of trial and error involved in coming up with successful fundraising schemes.

My next attempt was a Ceilidh, which I had begun organizing for the month of June, only two months away. Once again, I started asking local businesses to sponsor me or donate raffle prizes.

*

For a while I had noticed that I kept having blood in my poo. The trainee doctor told me it was just piles causing it. I carried on with my life and was busy working, modelling, training, fundraising and doing my City and Guilds in Youth Work. I tried to ignore it but the problem was not going away. Somehow I knew it wasn't piles. I asked my doctor to send me for tests.

She said, "You are worrying for nothing."

She told me, "Telephone for a colonoscopy appointment in two days' time."

Two days passed and I phoned to book an urgent appointment.

The receptionist said, "I have you down as a

routine case."

I'm not sure why I lied when I said, "I think it's urgent because there's a lot more blood and it's painful."

The truth is, I wasn't in pain but there was a lot of dark blood and mucus. I just felt that something wasn't right and I found myself crying. My hernia was causing me a great deal of pain too. She booked me in for two days later.

My son Jake and our friend Al took me to the clinic for the colonoscopy. Whilst the camera was up my 'Jacksie' I noticed the ugliest thing I had ever seen.

I commented to the doctor, "That doesn't look attractive."

He didn't reply immediately.

After the procedure he said, "You know that part that you said wasn't very attractive?"

"Yes," I said.

"I'm sorry...It's cancer."

He described the tumour, which was in my lower bowel, as being as big as an orange.

He went on, "I have taken biopsies but I don't need to wait for the results. It is definitely cancer. You need to be on the operating table within two weeks as it has ulcerated and is urgent."

It was the 23rd April and my birthday. I was diagnosed with colon cancer. What a lovely present!

I was frightened at that moment. I looked right into the doctor's eyes, willing him to say it wasn't cancer but it was and there was no taking it back. It felt ironic that the day was also Shakespeare's birthday and he had died on his birthday. I had lost a few of my friends to this terrible disease and now it had got me too. I couldn't believe it, I was only forty-four years old. More problems in my life, like I hadn't had enough already!

Jake and Al were in the waiting room and I was going to have to tell them.

I had to tell my son his mum had cancer.

I asked the doctor, "Can I keep this from my children?"

He said, "You must tell them the truth."

The Doctor went to get Jake. He immediately knew something was wrong. The look on his face when I told him will never leave me. He was about to be broken in two before my eyes.

The doctor said, "What your mum needs now more than anything, is for you to be strong for her."

Sure enough, at that moment he sucked all that emotion in.

"I will be," he said, bravely.

His eyes where burning into me, he was dying to cry but would not allow himself to break.

I said, "We can deal with this."

We left the building and drove home. On the way, my local surgery called my mobile to ask me to go straight to see my doctor. She was sorry she had failed to diagnose my cancer earlier and told me what would be happening next. I tried to take in all the information about scans and tests I would be having. At that moment I realized that I was going to have to make changes to my life. It felt like a joke but at the same time, it wasn't funny. I had been sitting in front of people in white coats telling me I might die (or so I thought).

What the hell was going to happen now?

I hadn't told my daughter Ella yet. There was still this hurdle to overcome. I am glad, although I shouldn't say this that my son went into our house before me and told her.

All I heard was her screaming and crying.

"No, no, no, you're kidding me, Jake you're lying!"

I was fighting back tears in the kitchen but was determined that when she saw me I was going to be absolutely strong and fine. Ella telephoned her dad.

He told her, "I have never met a woman as strong as your mum," reassuring her and Jake that I would be okay. This was the start of us rebuilding our lives once again.

*

From childhood through to being a teenager, I was physically, mentally and sexually abused by my father. I survived that alone, without family support. If a stranger had raped me, I would at least have had the support of my family. I had to be tough and make close friends, who I substituted for my family.

I ran away from my dad's house at fifteen years old and grew up quickly to survive. I went to my mum's house. However, I found myself at aged sixteen with my own rented house. I had no choice but to be tough again. My mum had kicked me out because she couldn't cope with my hormones.

She said, "I have done my job as a parent. You're on your own now."

She told me: "When you'd had enough of being treated like an adult by your dad, you came back to me. What the hell did you expect me to do about it? "

My dad broke my heart and now my mum was breaking it.

I lived alone with my children for thirteen years, their father refusing to take responsibility for their upbringing. My children were solely dependent on me whilst he was making his millions. He paid the least he could get away with after I left him and still pays me peanuts now.

He made my life hell.

By trying to get at me, he emotionally hurt our children in the process and still hurts them now. Despite this, I have managed to raise my son and daughter, through both difficult and brilliant times.

The diagnosis of cancer had turned my life upside down, especially with my climb approaching and Ella and Jake being upset. It was the last thing I needed. Still, it was only April and the climb would be in the following February.

I never gave up hope!

I read a book called, *Cancer Is Just A Word.* It inspired me to get on with my life and conquer the disease. All my life I struggled to keep my head above water, why would I not be able to survive this too? I decided to carry on as usual.

My kids would occasionally have melt downs.

They'd say, "It's all right for you, you can deal with it and you expect us to be like you all the time!"

How hard it was to find the answers when I looked at their frightened faces. It was difficult to try and stay positive for them and me. It felt like I was climbing a mountain before I'd even started, I can tell you!

I kept telling myself this *was* really happening to me. When people asked how I was, I told them I had cancer; it was as if I had to convince myself it was real and I just couldn't make it fit me.

I had scans and tests and emptying my bowels for them was horrid but I just got on with it, without fuss. Ella was in the middle of her GCSE exams and I didn't want to stress her more than necessary.

I saw various doctors and was blessed that my friend Al was taking me to every appointment. He helped me to take in everything that was explained. They said the cancer had nothing to do with my current diet but I changed over to a Ketogenic one anyway. My friend, Andy, helped me with this diet which cuts out carbohydrates, in order to starve the cancer.

I was chasing up appointments from the separate departments and it was a good job I did, otherwise my waiting time would have been longer. It took five, long, scary weeks in all before I was under the knife. When the day of the operation arrived, 31st May, I felt ready and strong enough to conquer this latest mountain. I arrived at the hospital that morning, not knowing whether I would wake up again, whether they would be able to remove all the cancer or whether I would be pooing into a bag for the rest of my life. I was still single and my two children were completely dependent on me. They were my whole world. I wasn't ready to leave the planet yet, I had too much to do and see.

My daughter and Al came with me. They were both there when the surgeon told me the worst outcome would be death, because if the joining of the bowel wasn't sealed properly it would leak and poison me. I could see Ella was starting to show signs of not keeping her emotions together, as she had tears in her eyes. Al left with her at that moment and we hugged and kissed each other, feeling apprehensive and scared but courageously remaining positive and strong.

My surgeon, Dr Fawole, came to my hospital bed, to take me to theatre. He looked as handsome as always with his cheeky-boy, big smile and professional manner. We walked together and I wished him luck. He smiled and chuckled back at me before going to scrub up ready for me to be anesthetised. He looked like president Obama. All the nurses and patients would say so, but I knew he was far more handsome and clever.

My operation lasted nine hours, which was gruelling for the Jake and Ella. I woke up in recovery to a pleasant nurse making sure I was comfortable, telling me everything had gone well. I was full of tubes and wired up to machinery, but **no colostomy bag!** I was happy. After a while my surgeon and anaesthetist team wheeled me into the Intensive Care Unit (ICU).

I couldn't help myself from singing, "I'm H.A.P.P. Y. I'm H.A.P.P.Y. I know I am, I'm sure I am, I'm H.A.P.P.Y."

I sang it at the top of my voice all the way through. My surgeons were laughing, saying in all their years nobody had ever sung to the heavens like that. I was so happy to be alive and to not have a bag. In the end, I didn't go to ICU, because when they saw my high spirits they changed their minds and transferred me to the High Dependency Unit. (HDU).

Dr Fawole had carefully positioned me on a pressure-relieving mattress to make sure I was as comfortable as possible. I was impressed tremendously with his care and attention and glad I had chosen him to be my surgeon. I first met him for a consultation in Wakefield Hospital and liked his appearance and professionalism. When he said he was referring me on to someone else in the hospital, I said I would prefer him to do my procedure.

He replied, "I don't operate at Wakefield, only at Dewsbury, which is further away for you."

I told him, "I don't care about the distance."

I thought to myself, *there is no way I am coming back here for an operation.* I had lost total faith in

Wakefield after the bad experience of my hernia operation. I told him that I had two teenage children and that I was the only person in the world they could rely upon. They needed me! I told him how I had started raising money for a charity to climb Kilimanjaro in eight months' time.

He said, "If you take my name to the very top, I will make sure I get you up there." He smiled and agreed to operate. I was now smiling too. What a guy hey? My hero!

Recovery was slow and very painful, to say the least and staying in hospital for a week had its highs and lows. It was an experience I'm sure never to forget! For a start, the first night I couldn't sleep, even with all the drugs and morphine in me. I nodded off and woke to blood-soaked sheets, blankets and nightie. This scared me: I thought I had haemorrhaged but it turned out that the cap had come off the cannula inserted in the back of my hand.

"Why won't you go to sleep?" The nurse asked.

I said, "I am scared the join on my bowel hasn't sealed properly and I could be being poisoned to death as we speak."

She asked me, "Have you passed wind yet?"

I replied, "Yes."

"So it's worked then," she said. "Imagine your bowel like a balloon, if it hasn't sealed there would be no wind."

I was impressed with her explanation and from then on I appreciated being able to fart until my heart was content! I hadn't had a poo yet, though and that was scary. Because my tumour had been the size of an orange, faeces couldn't pass properly and Dr Fawole said he'd never seen as much backed up in anyone before. Though I still hadn't got to the stage that I felt I could go.

My friends brought my children to visit me and although they were relieved that the operation seemed to have gone well, I could tell from the look on their faces they were frightened. My face was swollen from the anaesthetic and I was covered in wires and tubes. There was still a long way to go before I was completely recovered but we were overjoyed to be back together again.

After three days I was told I would be moving onto a ward. This meant I would have to be separated from my comfy bed with remote control. I begged them to let me take it with me because I was frightened I would not be able to get comfortable on an ordinary mattress, due to the persistent pain. Unfortunately, I was not allowed because these beds were only for use in ICU and HDU.

Two lovely nurses came to transfer me downstairs

on to another ward and I said I would prefer to walk and take the stairs. They looked at each other in surprise.

"Ok then," they agreed and we slowly and painfully descended to what was going to be my new home for a few days.

Steadily I was helped into bed and was wired up again. The process had tired me and I needed to sleep, as my visitors would soon be there. I was still administrating my own morphine and was dozing off with my curtains pulled around, so I could only hear and not see what was going on. Suddenly I heard a loud voice, which seemed to be coming from a woman in the bed opposite. She wouldn't stop talking and just wouldn't shut up. Every few seconds she would shout across to other patients who were not really responding and were trying their best to ignore her. I thought to myself, *oh my god, how am I supposed to rest with her shouting her useless mouth off every two seconds?*

She made sleep impossible so finally I asked her to keep the noise down.

I told her I had just come from HDU and needed to rest. I have never heard such a boom box of filth in my life.

She started shouting at patients and staff.

"Who the fuck does she think she is?" She wailed. She said she'd been on the ward three weeks and nobody had ever complained or told her to keep her big gob shut.

I replied, "Probably because nobody dare say anything, but I'm asking you to please keep the noise down, I need to rest."

By this time nurses had heard the noise and came to my bed. They said she was always this loud and was doing everyone's heads in with her constant demands. Other patients were listening and my adrenalin was pumping. The woman had really unnerved me and I wasn't sure what she would do next. After all, I wasn't in a position to knock her out if she came at me through the curtains. She carried on grumbling and swearing for a while but did lower her tone a bit.

When I was brought onto the ward, I spotted the toilet was miles away, at the far end. *What a nightmare, I wanted my own toilet!* While she was eating her dinner the loud-mouth woman was going on about how she hadn't been for a crap for three weeks. It didn't stop her complaining there wasn't enough food, though. She even shouted at her poor husband who'd brought their kids to see her. I could hear that he had brought lots of chocolate goodies for her which she devoured. Lying there I thought to myself, *all that's got to come out and I'm not sharing a toilet with you when it does.*

All of a sudden, the ward was empty of nurses

because they had been called to an emergency meeting. When they returned they told us that the entire ward would be shutting down and that we would be moved onto other wards. No explanation was given. The nurses opened my curtains and, low and behold, I saw the fattest giant haystack of a mess I had ever seen looking at me from opposite. I was bloody glad to be getting out of there, I can tell you!

The nurses wheeled me to my new room, which looked onto the nurse's station. I had my own en-suite bathroom. I was buzzing because this meant I could potter around in peace with all my lovely gifts and go to my own loo in privacy. I was glad because it wasn't long before my time came to use the loo. I surely thought I would die after parting with a log which you could have kept the fire going with for a week! It had been extremely painful and I dreaded the next time. I asked the doctor for laxatives and suppositories and got them, along with more pain relief.

The nurses were really kind and helped me settle into my new room. I got the impression that the move had happened because they could sense trouble ahead and felt that separating me from the loud woman was for the best. I didn't need this extra stress.

From my room I was able to watch the comings-and-goings of the patients and nurses. I could see the rude and loud woman, along with her friend, who was also a patient, going from bed to bed, pestering others who were clearly dreading the pair coming to them.

One night the friend unexpectedly appeared in my room. She delighted in telling me her cancer had started in her bowel, like mine. She now had a colostomy bag and was fed through a drip. She told me horror stories about how her cancer had spread to many places and how she had to have it cut out. She looked like the ghost who said, "Get off my train!" in the movie Ghost! It was scary and I was letting her get to me, until the staff nurse came in and told her to get out.

The nurse said, "I am sorry, I should have kept an eye on her to prevent her coming into your room." Apparently the woman regularly visited other patients, telling them of her ailments.

The nurse tried to put my mind at rest, saying, "The same won't happen to you. There is a name for people who enjoy spreading bad news, they are called **witch** patients."

I felt sorry for the nurses because the two friends would bully them to give them morphine. The nurses were reluctant to administer it, because they did not appear to be in pain. I had noticed them regularly disappearing down the stairs for a cigarette, making arrangements to meet up for the next fag break. The two women kept arguing with the nurses and threatening to go to a higher authority if they were refused the pain relief. Guess what? The selfish couple did make a complaint to the doctors, which resulted in the nurses feeling more pressured and giving into them.

On one occasion, when Maya was visiting, a nurse came into my room to escape for a few minutes and we would laugh and joke to try and lighten the mood. What was most annoying was that there were other patients on the ward who were seriously ill and more deserving of the nurse's care and attention. They were the ones who really needed pain relief.

After only two nights in my side room, I was moved on to a ward as they required my room for a lady who had a sickness bug and needed to be quarantined away from the main ward. I was disappointed, but the ward they moved me to was occupied with lovely, older ladies. We had a laugh and some of the patients even sponsored me for my climb. The old ladies were funny and kept trying to hook me up with the doctors, who were doing their rounds.

I was surprised at how much pain relief I still needed. When I mentioned my pain to Dr Fawole he asked me which side it was on and when I pointed to it, he explained that it was where the camera had been.

He gently and playfully punched me on the other side and I told him, "I owe you one!"

He replied, "Wait until you're fitter and we're on an even playing field." I thought to myself, I am going to miss his sexy highness when I go home.

The son of a sweet, senile, old lady came to visit next to me and was flirting and asking for my number. I gave it to him and as soon as he had left, he sent me a red rose via text message and asked me on a date. Oooooooo, the old ladies were over the moon, as they couldn't understand why I was still single, a lovely girl like me!

After seven days I was discharged and ready to go home. I said my tearful goodbyes to my new found friends and we hugged each other and wished each other good health.

Even the nurses cried and said, "You have been the least bother of them all."

Al came to take me home.

Just a few days later, I put on my blue and white, spotted gypsy summer dress and Gary, my date from the hospital, picked me up looking like Keanu Reeves in the film *The Matrix*, posing in his black shades and fast black car. We drove to the Cow n Calf on Ilkley Moor. It was a beautiful summer's day. I was treated to expensive wine and food while sitting out in the hot sun, overlooking Yorkshire's stunning countryside. Gary was a handsome fella but when I found out he didn't pay maintenance to his three kids, I went off him. Never mind, it was a relaxing place to be, after all I'd been through and we had an enjoyable drive in his sporty car.

I asked the nurses in hospital to show me how to

inject my lower tummy with Warfarin, as it had to be done daily for a month. I didn't want the district nurses coming every day, I was impatient to get on with normal life. After a while, Ella wanted to practice giving me injections, as she is training to be a veterinary surgeon, so I let her.

Ten days after returning home from hospital the nurse came to remove my clips. The incision where they had brought the tumour out had not healed properly and there was a hole, which she had to pack. Then there were more metal clips to remove from the three other incision sites. Yuck! I bloody hated that, I looked like a patchwork doll.

Arriving home to my ever-demanding teenagers meant I would have to start getting on with life as quickly as possible.

Ella and her friend Chloe had arranged for us to do The Race for Life and it was scheduled to take place only three weeks after I had left hospital. We all dressed in pink outfits and they helped me hobble around Pontefract Racecourse to complete 5k. I had been able to run around last year. Receiving our medals at the end was an emotional and proud moment and we raised £400 for cancer research.

I would have to wait eight long weeks to find out if the surgery had been successful. My tumour had to be frozen and dissected and tests carried out on it, to determine whether it had spread to my bowel wall.

I went to Hope Valley in the Derbyshire Dales, just four weeks after surgery. It's what I call my second home and I wanted to recuperate by the side of the beautiful river. I drove on my own and towed my caravan. I really shouldn't have been driving but I just needed to get away. I cried all night, the first night I arrived, I was in so much pain. I phoned Janet, my colon specialist, the next morning. I was afraid I had done some damage by driving the one and a half hours to get there, with my feet pressing down on the peddles. I was losing a lot of blood and thought I was haemorrhaging. Thankfully, it was only my period starting, nothing more serious.

The pain settled down with the help of tablets. I could hobble about there and it was the best place for me to gradually begin my training, in readiness for walking up and down in the pool at my gym again. I had to start somewhere if I was going to meet the targets I had set for my climb.

I stayed in Hope Valley for a week, surrounded by beautiful rolling hills that cut into the deep valley. My friends, Joris and B, who own the camp-site, would visit me and collect my shopping from the supermarket. I was spoilt by everyone on site, in particular, my friend Jez, the landlord of the Old Bowling Green who brought me home-made pizza and wine. All my friends contributed in some way to making my stay as pleasant as possible.

Holidaymakers from the camp-site, local churchgoers and acquaintances from surrounding villages all sponsored my climb.

Eight weeks later I returned to the hospital with Al to see Dr Fawole, taking him a good bottle of wine and a card.

I wrote in it, *thank-you for saving my life. I still owe you one!*

I took chocolates for his registrar, Janet. They both sat with us and explained that the surgery had been a success. Luckily, the cancer had been contained within 1mm of my bowel wall and he was hopeful he had removed it all.

I cried with joy.

However, Dr Fawole wanted me to have chemotherapy: my biggest nightmare. I dreaded having this treatment because I had heard both good and bad reports about it. I was shocked that I was going to have to jump over more hurdles. Having to make more life threatening decisions was not what I had been expecting, for some reason. I was in shock and scared at the latest news. Taking thank-you cards and chocolates onto the ward straight afterwards was emotional. All the nurses were wishing me well for my climb, whilst I was once again unsure about my future.

As I suspected, when I went to see my chemo' specialist he told me the treatment would damage my heart organ, could give me another cancer, would compromise my immune system, I would lose my hair and be vulnerable to numerous illnesses. After six weeks treatment morning and night it couldn't even be guaranteed that the cancer would be destroyed. The specialist told me there was a three percent chance the cancer was still in my body and that chemo' could only reduce it to a two percent chance, meaning they could not guarantee it could take it away totally.

It was a lot to consider and I didn't feel able to make the decision about chemotherapy there and then. I needed time to think it through. The specialist gave me three weeks to make my mind up.

During this time I towed my caravan to Rainbow Camp near Ashbourne, in the beautiful Derbyshire Dales. This is a healing camp where you re-enact how the Native Americans lived close to nature. Alternative therapies are administered in teepees and yurts. It was a place I had been going for years with my children and I had many friends there. Ella came with me on this trip.

The decision about having treatment weighed heavily on my mind and I would get upset and angry that I had to make this choice. I had listened to friends' opinions and tried to take in all the advice and information but was getting nowhere. I decided to just put it to one side for a while and I made a conscious decision to start enjoying our holiday, being close to nature and alongside the rivers where I felt at peace.

After arriving back home, I knew I couldn't delay any longer. It was time to talk to Jake and Ella about the pros and cons of having the treatment. Of course, one of the cons was that I would not be able to do the Kilimanjaro climb. After much discussion, we decided against it.

I was feeling as well as could be expected and excited, once more, about my climb. Meanwhile, I was awaiting the next colonoscopy scheduled for twelve weeks after my operation. The removal of the cancer had made it possible for the camera to see further up my bowel. My scan did show more polyps further up my colon, but these were removed during the colonoscopy procedure.

*

June came and The Roisin Ceilidh Band was booked to perform at the Carlton Grange. I advertised the event in the Pontefract and Castleford local paper and Maya designed posters, which we put up everywhere. This time I sold tickets rather than just relying on people turning up.

On the night people bought raffle tickets which my friend, Catherine, was selling on the door. The band, generously performed for free, got everyone involved. The caller got three groups of eight people into a circle joining hands, dancing up and down the room, through each other's arms, then back round. There was a bar and after a few drinks we all had a tasty pie-n-pea supper and then danced again until 11.30pm.

It was great to see my friends who had come along to support the Laila Milly Foundation, this wonderful, much-needed cause in our area. It was not only friends who had been generous and kind: many other people came too. Everyone kept me positive and I felt a lot of love, which I needed more than ever at that time. After paying for the supper and the room, which was donated at half price, we raised £350.

The evening was a success and everyone had enjoyed themselves but things where getting tougher and I needed to think of another fund raising idea fast!

Money was coming in from sponsors, friends, my gym, the village churches and local businesses, but it was still not enough. To make matters worse, there were now only three of us taking part in the climb: Steve1, Steve2 (who was Steve1's best friend from school) and myself. Steve2 was not fundraising, he was paying for his own climb. This left me and Steve1 to raise money, meaning the charity would not receive much if we didn't pull our finger out!

Everyday I said to people, "I'm climbing Kilimanjaro to raise money for the Laila Milly Foundation. Would you like to sponsor me?"

Occasionally people would offer before I asked.

My next idea for a fundraising scheme was to put on a Laila Milly Christmas party. I asked a local pub if they would hold the event and a friend from church, called Ady, who has a local band, *The Masters Of Mellow,* agreed to play for free. In addition, I planned an auction and a raffle for the evening, booked for 5th December. This meant I had to encourage local businesses in Ackworth, Hemsworth, and some from further afield to donate gifts to be auctioned. Mick Hollinworth, the world-famous caricaturist, who had previously been very generous, gave free sittings. Jeremy, my friend and personal trainer, donated a lawnmower from JC Power Tools; two local hairdressers donated haircuts and products; Hinitt's, a local baker donated a voucher for a cake; Aldridge's Opticians donated a pair of glasses and £50; Simon from the gym in the village gave away a free membership and Big Baps and the Spread Eagle at Darrington helped to raise £300.

Many other businesses gave generously and I had collected lots to auction. I advertised in the local paper and we produced some brilliant posters and flyers which I posted out, along with information about the Laila Milly foundation. I gave loads of these to the landlord of the local pub where the Christmas party would be held, in order for him to leave on the bar and hand out to his customers.

The pub was my old local. Although not a local girl, (originally from Barnsley, I used to live with my two children at that end of the village on the Ackworth Park Hall and Farm. It had once been the grandest estate in the village, owned in the 1800's by the very fine John Gully, who was a prize fighter (boxer), horse racer, notorious gambler and politician. Born in 1783 and died 1863, he was a Catholic and had twenty-four children.

I asked the landlady if the Christmas tree would be erected in time and she said it would. Everything seemed to be coming together and I felt it was going to be a lovely event, with the local community supporting this great cause.

The night came and I dressed-to-kill, wearing a fitted Christmas party dress. As I walked into the pub two handsome guys called me over and said how beautiful I looked. They gave £20, just like that. I thought, *what a good start*. I had not charged for tickets, it was just going to be donations on the door.

My friend Catherine helped me to sell raffle tickets and was my treasurer again, as she had been for my Ceilidh. I set the auction prizes out and a few of my friends started arriving. My kids and Stuart were also there. I was so happy, thinking, *this is gonna be a great night,* but gradually, I realised that no one else was coming in, not even all the locals who usually crowded that pub every day. I talked to the staff serving behind the bar and they said they heard nothing about the charity event. I found this strange because the landlord had telephoned to ask how many guests would be coming, in order that he could arrange for the right amount of bar staff. I told him I wasn't sure but was hoping for quite a few, because I had advertised it well. Disappointingly, not one of my posters or leaflets about the charity was on display in the pub and consequently, virtually no one was there.

The band played and the few who did come were happy listening to great music and Christmas Carols, but the pub was nearly empty. At 10pm, the landlord told me he asked the band to stop playing and go home as my guests and I were preventing his locals from coming in, thus spoiling their normal routine!

I felt hurt.

I think the landlord knew no one else was coming in. I could not believe the mean spirit of some people but perhaps I should have known better! I was so disappointed with him at this point and felt my party had been sabotaged. I originally asked him if I should put on a buffet and he said no, people would not come for food, they would be coming for the event. Now he was saying that the reason nobody had come was because there was no food available.

Nevertheless, we had fun drawing the raffle just after 10pm and the winners won flowers, wines and chocolates, which had been kindly donated. The auction didn't go ahead and the donated items had to be packed back into the car. I would quickly have to think of another idea to use them.

My friends and children tried to keep my spirits up; Jake, Catherine and I went to the Boot-n-Shoe pub and raffled-off a meat hamper, which a local, friendly butcher, Ivan, had given. This raised £100.

The deadline for raising the money for the climb was only fifteen days away. I had raised £1000 over ten months, but still needed £1500. Some of the sponsor money would not be coming in until I had completed the climb.

I was beginning to panic.

If I didn't have the money within two weeks, I would be unable to make the booking and I would have to tell everybody that I wasn't doing the climb after all. I would have felt bad and compelled to give the sponsor money back. Not only this, my dream to climb my mountain would not come true!

I was still swimming at the gym four times a week but wasn't sure if my fitness was up to scratch. I'd sometimes see Steve1 there and he asked if I raised the money yet.

"No," I said.

"Do you have a plan B?" He asked.

"No," I replied, "because plan A will work."

"What if plan A doesn't work? Have you got any savings or family to borrow from?"

I answered, "No".

He told me he had been unable to raise the money and was having to pay for himself, meaning that he and his family would not be able to afford a holiday this year. He was saying he wished he had not booked it now, with all the bother it was causing. It made me wonder if he was saying that because there was only me left raising money!

Ten days left and Stuart came up with the idea to ask the local Co-Op if I could raffle off the remaining auction prizes in their supermarket, which I thought was a miracle.

I power-dressed in my Boss winter suit and heels and asked to see the manageress. Although the manageress wasn't in that day, the assistant manageress asked if she could help. She was a lovely lady and I told her my story and we both had tears in our eyes as I left her with information about the charity.

Two days later I went back and saw the manageress.

She said, "We don't do charity promotions in December because we are so busy."

However, because I had told her about my battle with cancer and my determination to do the climb and raise money and awareness, she said, "You can have a table at the front of the store and sell your tickets, for as long as you like."

It was decided that I would be there for five days.

My prayers were answered. I sat everyday in my big, winter coat, freezing.

I would say to everyone who passed, "I am climbing Kilimanjaro for the Laila Milly Foundation. Do you want to buy a raffle ticket?"

I must have said it a million times and nearly all the customers bought or gave generously. People would stop and chat as they passed, willing me on with their Christmas spirit and cheer.

At night Stuart and I would count the money: I was raising around £200 to £300 a day and it was coming to the weekend so the supermarket would be getting busier. My vision of climbing my mountain was still in sight.

On Sunday, the fifth day, I drew the raffle just before the store closed. I had written names and telephone numbers on every ticket and was very pleased to announce the winners. I thanked everyone for their kindness and I personally delivered the prizes to their homes. I counted the donations for the last time and low and behold, I was only £200 short.

We bagged all the notes and coins and filled a rucksack full to the top. I took it to the bank with Maya the next morning. The bank staff re-counted it and I put the final £200 in from my own pocket. If I hadn't got the money now, I wouldn't be going up my mountain, but I had achieved my goal and my adventure was about to begin.

PART 3

My Safari - Another Dream Come True

I had seen the Serengeti in my book, *The Land Extreme Earth*. It was the largest National Park in the world (14,750km sq) with the most wildlife on Earth.

I knew that whilst in Africa I needed to take the opportunity to go on a Safari. I realized that I may never get the chance again and I just wasn't sure if my health would let me down in the future. I had to make it happen, it was an opportunity of a life time.

I saved a portion of the money toward the cost of the four day Safari, but only one week before my adventure in Africa was about to start, I didn't have enough money. With the deadline for booking approaching fast, it seemed far out of my reach.

I had to beg and borrow the remaining money from good friends, Phil, Jeremy, Jan and Al, who were happy to lend it. The booking was made and I felt like the luckiest girl on Earth. This was going to be a totally different kind of wonder from Mount Kilimanjaro.

While Sunning myself in my bikini round the Keys

Hotel pool, I was totally chuffed looking back on what I'd achieved in the past year and my mind soon moved into the present day as African people strolled in the hotel garden. They were very polite and would stop for a brief chat, before carrying on with their business, whilst I relaxed the afternoon away, dipping in and out of the pool.

Being friendly, I said hello to a local guy and asked him to take a picture of me larging-it-up, drinking a Malibu and pineapple, wearing my big shades, looking like Sophia Loren. I chatted with him about my climb and asked him if he knew King Charles, who I knew lived nearby. It turned out he came from the same village and he said everyone knew him because he liked a good laugh. A lot like me! I was feeling very proud to know King Charles and glad that he had been the guide to lead me to the summit.

The sun was beginning to set and as I could feel the evening chill coming, I went up to my room to shower and change for the evening meal. There was one window in my room, quite high up, that looked out into the hotel's small backyard. Earlier that afternoon I had stood on my bed to look out the window to see the view. I saw maids washing my clothes on a scrubbing board, like in the olden days and pegging them out to drip dry.

It was an old single bed on legs with a mosquito net hung over it from the ceiling. It touched my face when I lay down and I didn't like it, so I got up and stretched it out as much as I could and tucked it under my mattress to keep it off me! The room was clean, small and basic and, although there was no way it could be classed as a five star hotel, the atmosphere was warm and friendly, which mattered more to me. It was not like I would be staying in it long. There was too much else to see.

I put on my sandals and summer dress (yes, my luxuries had returned), ready to go downstairs to dinner. I wondered whose company I would occupy my time with this evening.

The hotel reception and dining room were very quiet; I was told most of the guests had gone to climb Kilimanjaro. I thought how extremely ghostlike it was for a hotel and I felt alone. Calling home for only the second time and talking to my son Jake made me miss my children and I wished we could have shared this experience, like we had shared so many before. I had my book with me but wasn't interested in reading because my attention was held by my surroundings and by watching the staff and the few locals that passed by.

I was kept entertained by the unusual décor of mural paintings depicting Maasai tribes, living in their mud huts, the woman carrying baskets on their heads, the men carrying spears in their hands, wrapped in brightly coloured blankets.

I placed my food order. Burger, chips and coke: my body craved carbs'. There were also murals of elephants and giraffes beneath the beautiful, snowy summit of Kilimanjaro. All this gave me some idea of what I would see the next day. The staff were friendly, smiling and chatting and, after dinner, I decided to go to the bar for a nightcap.

In the bar I got talking to a white African man, John, who had his own safari business called *The Wild Frontiers*. He was with his friend and work colleague. John asked me if he could buy me a drink and I politely asked for a Quantro on ice. It was delicious, especially after having had no luxuries for ten days.

We chatted and I told some bad jokes like, "I bumped into a dyslexic Yorkshire lass the other day, she was wearing a cat flap on her head" and "two blondes walk into a building, you'd think one of them would open the door." (Please don't take offence, I am also Dyslexic, Yorkshire and Blonde).

John admitted that I had got him with the cat flap joke and laughed. It was a pleasant evening meeting new people and having a laugh. I was feeling great. Another positive aspect was that John-of-The-Wild Frontiers has put me in contact with his friend who is a vet in the Tanzanian wild life parks. My Daughter is training to be a vet and dreams of shadowing one in

Africa. After enjoying the evening I retired to my room tired, but excited at the prospect of my Safari.

Day 1
25th Feb 2014

Waking up to the hot sunshine was lovely. I decided to eat breakfast outside overlooking the pool, where I was reunited with John and his colleagues. We chatted and ate a buffet style breakfast and fry up. It was scrumptious and no maize porridge, thank goodness!

Back in my room, I dressed in my cream mosquito-proof safari shirt, denim shorts and boots, with a khaki headband; I was definitely looking the part.

I packed all my belongings because I wouldn't be returning to the hotel after the Safari, as had originally been planned. I had lost a day due to all the delays at the beginning of my trip. Jagged Globe had to re-book everyone's flight back. That meant it would be a rush again at the end of the Safari, but it would be worth it! I had been in this beautiful country, surrounded by stunning mountains, lush greenery and colourful people for eleven days now and had loved every minute of it.

I packed up my army rucksack with the things I would need every day to survive the heat and mosquitoes. My two big holdalls (one containing my climbing gear) would travel with us every day in the

Ford Ranger. In my room, I left coffee and sweets for the hotel staff and tipped the laundry lady and the porter, who brought my bags down, five-thousand Tanzanian shillings each. It sounds a lot but its pennies to us (around £1.50), that's all I had. I asked someone to take pictures of us all stood together before I left and then we said our goodbyes.

At 8am I met a lady from Jagged Globe tourist company, who I'd been introduced to the day before. She gave me my itinerary for the next three days. I was told I wouldn't be going to the Serengeti after all because I had only three days left, not four and it was too far away. I felt a sad and disappointed because I specifically wanted to see the animal kingdom of the Serengeti, which I had seen in *The Land Extreme Earth*. I wondered if I would actually get to see any wildlife at all on my Safari. However, she told me I would visit two National Parks, Lake Manyara (325km sq) and Tarangire (2,850km sq) and the Ngorongoro Conservation Park (8,292km sq). I would be staying one night in a Safari lodge with spectacular views of the Ngorongoro Crater, On the second night, the rep' said, I would be sleeping in a tent lodge, guarded by an armed Maasai warrior who would protect me from unwanted predators.

On the last day I would be taking a night flight from Kilimanjaro to Amsterdam, followed by a connecting flight to Leeds & Bradford Airport.

I was introduced to my driver, Gibson, at 9am.

Goodbye to the warm friendly staff at the keys hotel before I set off on my safari.

Instantly he reminded me of a gentleman called Higgins in the TV series, *Magnum*. He told me that my guide taking me on Safari had been changed to someone called Nelson, who we had to pick up in Arusha. I couldn't believe it and knew at once it was Nelson, one of the guides from my climb. He had told me he was travelling from Mount Kilimanjaro to Arusha where he lived. I remember, because I thought Nelson said he was going to Russia and I recall thinking he had a long way to go home! Another blonde moment. That was a good start, I knew my guide.

Gibson and I set off on our way to Arusha City, which was two and a half hours away. I loved being driven through the heart of Africa, surrounded by bright sunshine and ever changing mountain scenery. Once again, I observed how people lived their everyday lives in the busy towns and villages, full of cars, cyclists and mini-buses which were jam-packed full with people. The streets were busy at this early hour with people going shopping, to work, church and school. It looked like modern Africa, compared to how the Maasai tribes lived. The long journey was tiring and I was unable to keep my eyes open, dozing in and out of shallow sleep.

En-route we passed lots of markets where people chatted, carrying baskets or bundles on their heads. Many women had babies strapped to their backs, this always fascinated me. The women carry themselves with dignity and composure looking beautiful and feminine in their colourful dresses. It's funny, but I never saw babies crying or children throwing themselves on the floor having tantrums. Gibson told me the children become independent as young as three years old and had to walk to and from school by themselves, sometimes up to 3km. We passed several children walking at the side of the road and they waved to us as we drove by, with big smiles and shouting 'karribu, karribu,' meaning *welcome*. They were so cute, you could see how healthy and happy they looked, dressed in their blue and green uniforms. They appeared well-cared-for, even though their housing and way of living is substantially poor compared to ours.

There were lots of smartly dressed older men and women wearing old fashioned, brightly coloured clothing. Large groups of younger people, not as smartly dressed, sat on motorbikes with their girlfriends, milling around outside shops, cafes and tin huts, all chatting and basking in the sun, without a care in the world. It made me think that there must be a lot of unemployment, probably because there is little or no industry.

As we drove, Gibson told me about the Maasai people who lived in small, round, mud huts in the countryside. He also pointed out other tribes, he could tell by their hair, shape of face or colour, who was from which tribe. The boys walked along the roadside with their cows or goats, waving a long stick, in order to control the herd, their slim bodies wrapped in blue and red blankets, looking very proud of their livestock. The

The Chewit Boys

cows are a symbol of their wealth and status and the more they have, the richer they are. Rather than selling a cow, which I was amazed to hear could be sold for $400, they would prefer to send the kids out begging for a living.

Gibson would complain about the children stopping us and begging for money as we slowed down for speed humps. He always did this in a humorous, kind way, which made me laugh. I took a picture of two Maasai boys and they wanted money from me for taking it. Instead, I gave them a packet of Chewits to share, but they were not impressed.

I told them, in jest, "It will save you going to the shop," because there aren't any shops for miles to go to, unlike back home.

We drove onto the dual carriageway, increasing our speed, but after a while we had to stop for me to use the toilet. This turned out to be a hole in the ground over which I struggled to get my aim right when squatting. We rejoined the highway and I dozed on and off again, eventually arriving in Arusha late morning.

As we passed through the outskirts of Arusha City, I saw plenty of poverty and what looked like a shanty town. As we drove further into the heart of the city, Gibson pointed out a big, white, grand building, which was the president's residence.

Soon we pulled up at a big, white building, which transpired to be the tourist company where Nelson worked.

I got out of the Ford Ranger to stretch my legs, looking around at the busy city, whilst Gibson went inside to look for Nelson. It was so different from the mountains and I was excited at the prospect of learning a lot more about Africa's culture and wildlife.

I smiled as I saw Nelson coming to greet me in his most flirtatious, gentlemanly fashion, flashing his brilliant white teeth and wide smile, which lit up his face. He looked fit, dark and handsome and was dressed to kill in his sexy cowboy boots, straight legged jeans and checked, fitted shirt, which showed off his fit physique and lean body, ripped with muscle. He was wise to dress correctly for a lady and I now had two gentlemen as my guides for the next three days.

Nelson was much younger than me, but still, I was only looking! We hugged and I said I was excited he was going to be showing me his country. I also told him that I was hungry, so we walked across the road to a café, me and my posse, where we enjoyed refreshments amongst his friends.

He had joked that his friends would ask, "When are you bringing a lady friend to see us from your adventures?"

And here I was, someone who was curious and

wanted to see the real culture of Africa.

We ordered delicious samosas, filled with mince and I tried a rubbery looking sausage which I couldn't chew, so I left that. As we left the cafe, I gave some money and a hug to a poor, badly maimed, disabled old man with no legs, who was begging on the street. We crossed the busy road, back to the Ford Ranger.

Arusha was fascinating. It felt surreal as I watched the people in the hot sun, surrounded by all the different smells and sounds. It reminded me that I was miles away from home, living my dream and lucky to be here. I was one of only a few white people and as I have white blonde hair, I stood out like a sore thumb and everyone stared at me as they walked past.

Nelson let me have the front seat. From the back, he pointed out things of interest as we passed villages.

He asked me, "What is your favourite animal, Carol, you want to see?"

I told him, "It's the giraffe, because of its great beauty, elegance, grace and strength."

He said, "That is very good, it is the emblem on the Tanzanian flag." He told me the crane was on the Ugandan flag.

Nelson was very knowledgeable and I was soon taking notes in my diary as we drove along the free-way to Manyara National Park.

We passed different tribes and I saw women washing their clothes in the rivers, beating them against the rocks. We talked about how some tribes migrated with their animals and worldly possessions and Nelson showed me the busy trading places where they buy supplies. He pointed out underground springs, where they go to collect water in the dry season. Not all the Maasai migrate, some of the swampland has enough water for them to settle permanently. Many tribes gather near the Mosquito River, where water and supplies are plentiful, enabling them to grow rice. I found it sad to see how their everyday living seemed to be taken up with just surviving.

It was fun listening to Nelsons calming, chilled voice, trying to make out what he was saying, enjoying his broken, sexy, African accent. He and Gibson would sometimes talk to each other in Swahili. I liked that too and would sometimes pick up on their humorous tone and laugh along with them, as I enjoyed watching the world go by.

We stopped at a safari camp-site for a picnic lunch which the Keys Hotel had packed up that morning. The camp-site had a pool and I thought, *Ooh I like this, I could stay here with Jake and Ella*. We had stayed on many camp-sites together in the past.

Although I knew Nelson, we hadn't chatted that much during the climb and I now struggled to keep the conversation flowing. I was tired from the constant travelling, we had driven 310km that day; I was in pain from my operation; stiff and sore from my climb and couldn't eat much due to the heat and feeling exhausted. Lunch was very pleasant though, sitting under a big umbrella together, shading from the mid-day sun and blistering heat, chatting and excited at the prospect of seeing wild animals.

Our journey continued and we took a left off the free-way, driving for about an hour, passing lush green countryside, surrounded by more stunning mountain views.

Manyara National Park 325km sq

The Lake Manyara Park entrance was huge, like the *Jurassic Park* film set. Baboons, some with babies hanging under their belly, were coming to have a nosey, hoping for scraps of food and trying to get into the bins that had been chained down. You can't feed them, though, or they'd never disappear. They were very entertaining and cute, waving their ugly, pink, shiny arses at me in disgust, for not feeding them.

At the entrance to the park, there was a museum full of interesting historical facts about wild animals, tribes, volcanoes and about how we have evolved to the present day. We took lots of photos, then drove

Baboons walking away with the hump after not being fed.

Love this sausage tree!

through the giant gates, taking us miles again before we started to see Blue Monkeys. I stood up in the Ford Ranger with my head popping out of the sun roof, feeling like royalty.

As we drove further I was amazed at the sight of the sausage trees, as Nelson called them. They were festooned with long, dangly, sausage-shaped pods. It was amazing! Nelson told me which different type of tree each animal liked to eat. There were lots of brightly coloured birds flying around, perching in the trees, making nests at the end of the branches where they were out of harm's way from snakes and other predators. It was beautiful and fascinating to see how every creature and plant had its own survival technique.

The park is vast and lush with green plant life. It was hot, but nevertheless not hot enough for some animals and trees to survive.

Gibson drove slowly along until he spotted a herd of elephants. He had to point them out to me at first, because they were camouflaged in the trees. Soon I was taking pictures of them and my eyes were getting used to picking them out, under trees, grazing in the shade.

I saw my favourite animal, the graceful giraffe, or 'Twiga,' as it is called in Swahili. She was just how I imagined, but it was a million times better to see her roaming free in the wild with her young, living amongst all the other animals.

There were wildebeest, antelope, prides of lions and a surprisingly large number of different species of gazelle. They reminded me of the deer family. There were zebras, which survive on open grassland and bush and are able to sleep while standing up by locking their joints. Their stripes reflect the heat.

We saw massive herds of buffalo. Nelson told me that when the males have mated and have reached old age, they become known as bachelors and are kicked out of the herd, because they no longer have any use. I thought, poor things, when I saw them roaming about following each other in small, separate, groups. It made me think that they must be missing their families.

The warthogs, hyenas and the lions, reminded me of my favourite movie, *The Lion King*.

From Lake Manyara we drove a couple of hours to the Ngorongoro Conservation Park. Nelson told me that between Arusha and Tanire, there is an area of Government-controlled land which stretches for hundreds of miles that can't be built on. This land is known as 'Pallowed To Tiail' and is patrolled by armed guards and kept as forest or game reserves. People of all nationalities come to the region to hunt. They pay vast amounts of money for the pleasure of killing wild animals, which boosts the local economy. I found this sickening.

As we neared the Safari Lodge Hotel, we stopped off to take in spectacular views, looking down into the Ngorongoro Crater that once stood as a volcano but had sunk into the ground, creating a huge haven and fertile habitat for a wide range of wild animals.

Nelson gave me binoculars and I could see an elephant family. We took pictures, both posing and having fun, along with Gibson, before setting off again for the lodge. I checked-in while the guys went to the staff quarters.

My room of glass windows had stunning views, overlooking the park. All-in-all, it was beautiful.

I was alone in my luxurious room, sipping a gin and tonic from the bar, whilst relaxing in my first bath in twelve days. It was lush and I couldn't wait for dinner. I talked to Jake, it was lovely to hear his voice and catch up. I missed him and Ella very much, especially our hugs and the feeling of closeness we have.

I enjoyed dressing for dinner in my high heels and short dress, showing off one of my best assets: my legs. I was aware of being watched as I walked into the bar, probably because I was alone and feeling a little self conscious. There was an African band playing, dressed like Zulu warriors, drumming and dancing. I headed straight for the restaurant and ate lots a different, tasty and colourful dishes, washed down with red wine. I took pictures and enjoyed the décor, sat by myself. I am

Looking into the Ngorongoro crater.

used to this, having travelled alone to different countries.

Towards the end of the evening, a foreign waiter came and sat down at my table and told me his life story and when the bar closed I said goodnight and went to my room. The cheeky sod telephoned the room, asking if I wanted company!

I said, "No, I am going to sleep," and put the phone down.

I then nodded off until 6.30am. As I woke, I was greeted by the beautiful African sun, in all its glory, brightness and warmth, heralding a new day in this wonderful country.

I showered and got ready for a splendid breakfast of freshly made pancakes and syrup, fresh fruit, tea and coffee, which I ate outside on the balcony, overlooking breath-taking views, soaking in the morning sunshine until my posse arrived at 8.00 am.

Day 2
26th Feb 2014.
The Ngorongoro Conservation Park 8,292 sq km.

As we drove down into the bottom of the crater, Gibson stopped the Ford Ranger and told me it was okay to get out amongst the zebras to take pictures. I knew danger wasn't far away because they told me hippos, white rhino, lions and lionesses were in the

With the zebras.

Being brave, with danger close by.

Lions

area. I played it cool and posed for more shots. What an adventure this was turning out to be.

Within the conservation park, Nelson told me that multiple Maasai people live amongst the wild animals, along with their herds of livestock. The government keep a record of how many people live on the conservation park. They are allowed to graze and water their animals, but they can't cultivate maize, beans or other crops. The Government supply them with these. They use donkeys to go 20 to 30 km to collect wood and water. When the dry season comes, they migrate, as do the animals. Nelson told of how children have been eaten by lions, but it is rare.

We saw elephants, 'Tembo,' in Swahili, mingling in amongst the giraffes. Their leader 'Mtric,' pronounced Matrica, is the head of the elephant herd. There can be up to a hundred in the herd and the oldest takes care of them, leading them to water, food and shelter. They can live up to one-hundred years old. The elephants approached us, flapping their ears, a trick to make them look bigger. As they charged towards us, I didn't know if they were playing or trying to scare us off. The elephants surrounded the Ford Ranger. The bull elephant led the charge, they were huge and looked like giants compared to us. Without warning they stopped, turned and plodded off, to bask under the very large Baobab trees. The excitement of the amazing performance overwhelmed me, powerful yet gentle at the same time. Mother nature at her best.

As we drove further into the crater, we stopped and watched lions mating and took photos of their antics. I felt a little embarrassed when Nelson explained about the reproduction process. Although the mating only lasts for a minute, this can occur every ten minutes for up to three weeks.

In the distance a pride of lionesses lazed in the sunshine, whilst the cubs played and the head male stood guard, occasionally glancing towards the passing gazelle, eyeing up the potential prey. As we drove on, I became desperate for a pee and they stopped and told me to go at the back of the vehicle, which I did. I've never peed as fast. All the excitement was so much fun.

Driving on we came to a vast, magnificent lake, called Lake Makti, meaning soda lake. It is home to thousands of pink coral flamingos, and was a rare and spectacular sight to behold and offered a perfect opportunity to capture a beautiful image. They feed on alkaline water, migrating to Lake Natro or Lake Nakuru in East Kenya in order to survive when their food source here has been depleted.

Gibson stopped regularly for Nelson to point out all the different wildlife and my senses were aroused once again by all the different sights, smells and sounds of this wondrous park. It had been a mind blowing experience, but now it was time to leave, heading toward Tarangire National Park.

We drove through a town called Kisongo and it felt special to be chauffeured around, like Miss Daisy.

Nelson asked, "Would you like to see a Maasai village?"

I was excited. "Wow! Yes, please."

Nelson told me how the Maasai men can take between fifteen and twenty wives and how the women are friendly to each other. I simply could not comprehend this. They can have up to two hundred children between them, so the government builds a school in order for them to be educated. At age eight they go to Nanja, a government boarding school. When they leave after finishing A-levels, all the male teenagers have to join the military for three-to-six months to learn self-defence skills. This became law in 2012.

We arrived at the Masaai village and I was splendidly greeted by the tribal leader. He commanded the Maasai men to perform a traditional spiritual dance, jumping up and down with long sticks by their sides, chanting blessings from god. The ladies and the children joined in.

I was moved by the warm welcome and humbled by their simple lives. I joined in the dancing, feeling slightly embarrassed, but honoured to be included. The babies, who were strapped to their mum's backs, had flies on their faces, which made me feel sorry for them.

The tribal leader invited me into his hut, made of mud, straw and cow dung, (not before he asked me to marry him, I was flattered but told him I would prefer to stay single). He showed me the three tiny rooms they lived in, one for the mum and dad and one for the children to share and a room for the calves to keep warm. In the middle of the hut, which I didn't think was big enough even for one person, there was a small fire, and we had to crouch down to do everything. There were only slits in the walls for light. This highlighted how their way of life is a million times different from my own. He showed me a red jug made out of blood and milk.

I asked him, "What do you eat?"

He told me, "We eat goat and cows, but not vegetables."

I said, "You look good, considering you don't get your five-a-day."

We walked up the field to a small wooden school, packed with children of all ages and were greeted by excited shouts, "hello," big smiles and waving hands. The teacher had a baby strapped to her back and she asked a little girl to come out to the front of the class. She gave her a small stick and the girl pointed to the alphabet and some numbers on the blackboard, while all the other children recited and counted out loud. They sang for me and, once again, I was moved by their warmth and enthusiasm. I have worked in many schools and some things are the same wherever you are in the world. It just goes to show you don't need all the material things to make a good school.

After leaving the school, I was shown beautifully crafted items which the tribe created to sell. Brightly coloured jewellery, beautifully designed bags, dream catchers and talking sticks, which are used to pass round to the next speaker at a meeting or gathering and only the person holding the stick is allowed to talk. I bought a key ring, which I love and use every day.

The memories I took away, of meeting the tribe and visiting the school, will stay with me for the rest of my life.

Time was moving on and we still had a long way to drive, so we reluctantly left the village. The sun was setting and I asked Gibson if we could pull over, to take a picture, as this was to be my final sunset in this beautiful country. Once more, I was swept away by the majesty of this land.

Watching with emotion, I reflected on everything that had brought me to this place: the trauma of cancer, the huge effort of fundraising and the euphoric end to my climb. I had come through it all and felt that I was at peace with the world and Africa.

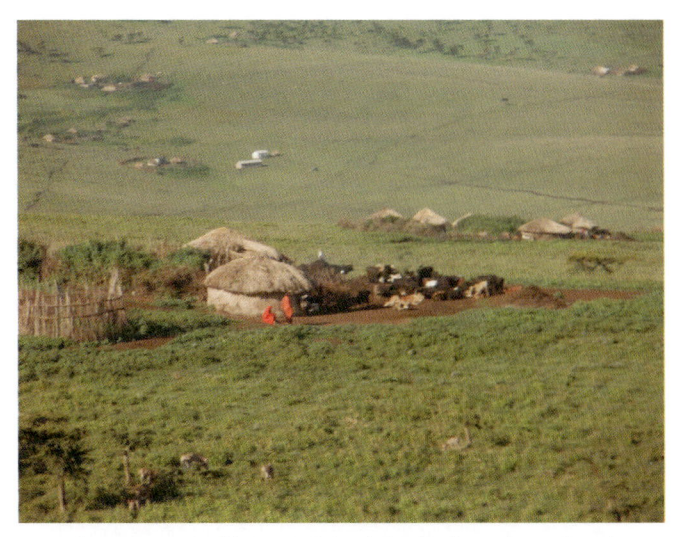

The Masaai village I visited, including the school.

Under the sun for the last time in Africa, made me feel at one with the world.

At 9pm we reached the tent lodge in Tarangire National Park. The days were long, crammed full with adventure and it was to be my last night in this awesome country. I asked Nelson and Gibson if they would join me for my last supper and they graciously accepted my invitation.

My tent lodge was completely unexpected and the inside of my room was beautiful, reminiscent of a fairy tale. I had a four-poster double bed, the posts were hand-carved in the form of the necks and heads of giraffes. It was draped with a pretty white and pink mosquito net. All the wooden furniture was carved into the shape of various animals.

I took a luxurious shower under a carved, king cobra shower head and dressed for dinner. An armed Maasai warrior guarded my room outside and waited to escort me to the restaurant, where the guys were waiting for me. We enjoyed talking about the differences in cultures and they told me what animals we would see in the Tarangier National Park. Nelson said this park is called the home of the elephant, which filled me with expectation.

He asked, "Do you want to visit a reptile centre tomorrow?"

I jumped at the chance. "Yes, of course. I'd love to."

My Masai warrior, guarding my tent lodge.

The centre was home to some of Africa's deadliest snakes, crocodiles, iguanas and other reptiles.

Nelson told me that, if I wanted to, on the way to the airport, I would have the opportunity to stop for gifts, to take back home.

The clear, starry evening and the lovely company, combined with the delicious food and wine, created a wonderful ambiance. It was late and I was exhausted and ready for bed, knowing that tomorrow would be another early start.

My armed guard escorted me back to my tent lodge, where he remained outside until the morning, protecting me from unwanted predators. I felt quite safe because I also had a whistle at my bedside. I prayed I wouldn't have to blow it.

Day 3
27th Feb 2014
Tarangire National Park. 2,850km sq.

This was the last day and final adventure. It was another beautiful morning and I ate breakfast, soaking up the sun, surrounded by the sparse vegetation, which had been singed by the sun's rays. The landscape was barren, compared to the lush greenery of the other parks.

The giraffes and elephants, living in harmony.

By 8am I was packed and ready to go, as previously instructed by Nelson. Gibson loaded the bags into the Ford Ranger for the last time. Nelson told me to cover up all my body today, otherwise I would be eaten alive by mosquitoes.

As we drove into the park, my eyes were once again filled with wonder at the site of emus, ostriches and packs of black jackals, which looked like ferocious wild dogs. We saw hartebeest, black rhinos, more zebras, lions and warthogs, who, because they have no neck, have to kneel down on their front legs in order to eat. We spotted more giraffes and many other birds and animals.

As promised, we saw lots of elephants that would take shade under the very large Baobab Trees. These trees could not survive in the Ngorongoro Crater, as it's too cold there, but very hot here. This came as a surprise to me, as I thought it felt hot everywhere.

Nelson pointed out the tree hyrax, a small squirrel-like animal, picking dung beetles out of elephant poo to eat for breakfast. Not very attractive but nonetheless interesting to see the food chain in action.

The elephants often wander out of the park boundaries in the dry season. This area is called the Bufa Zone. They go there in search of food and water as there is much competition from other animals in the park.

The park truly was the home of the elephants, as I saw many large herds with their cute babies, nestling under the Baobab Trees. Some of the trees had been stripped of bark and looked like skeletons. The Baobab stores water in its huge, sponge-like trunk, providing a valuable emergency supply for the elephants. It made me sad, because it brought home to me how they had to endure such hardship during dry season, throughout their lives.

I had a very dear friend called Lynn, who gave me a present of a carved elephant, bought in Africa on one of her many visits. My lovely friend, who was only in her forties, died last year of cancer. I now understand her passion for these animals. I will never forget them, or my friend.

The different species of animals, that I saw that day, were too numerous to mention. However, the white rhinos were a rare and wonderful sight. I felt lucky that I was able to photograph a pair in the distance. These amazing creatures are an endangered species and are protected.

Before lunch we came across hippos, wallowing in a large water hole, in the midday sun. It was an ideal place for us to have a picnic, surrounded by the spectacular mountainous scenery and of course, the noisy hippos. As we began to eat, it was necessary to take shelter practically sat underneath the vehicle. A flock of scavenging kite birds began to swoop down on us, attempting to steal the food from our hands. It was now my turn to be part of the African food chain.

We left the park and headed for the reptile centre, which was many miles away en route to the airport. We stopped at a gift shop, for refreshments and to buy souvenirs. There were lots of wooden carvings, intricately sculptured which must have taken years to craft. I wanted to buy some of the exquisite Tanzanite jewellery but couldn't afford it. After buying a few trinkets for family and friends, we continued our journey.

The Reptile Centre.

On entering the centre, I was introduced to the guide who showed me around the enclosure. He named the different kinds of snakes and pointed out those that were the most deadly, including the black mamba, African python, king cobra and many other colourful varieties. Without warning, the guide leapt into an open enclosure and picked a pale cream and white snake out of a tree and draped it around my neck, completely surprising me. I was about to panic, then realised if it didn't hurt him, then it wouldn't hurt me.

I soon became comfortable with the snake and had pictures taken of us staring into each other's eyes and I even gave it a kiss, my one and only amorous encounter in Africa! I also had pictures taken of me holding a sweet looking tortoise.

The only amorous encounter in all my time in Africa.

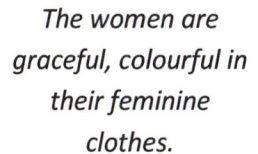

The women are graceful, colourful in their feminine clothes.

We moved on to the crocodiles and alligators. The differences were explained to me as they lay in the sun, with their tough, leathery, carved-out, prehistoric bodies and large, white, sharp teeth. I thought to myself, *I'm not kissing you mate*. My final encounter with the African wildlife!

Time was not on our side and Gibson had to drive at speed in order to reach our destination, the airport. We had planned to stop off in Arusha for a beer and to meet Nelson's friends in order to celebrate my time in Africa. Instead, we pulled over where Nelson's friend was waiting to run up to a hut bar to get us two very strong, tasty beers made from bananas. We drank these as we sped off again.

We arrived in the nick time for my flight and hurriedly said our goodbyes. We hugged and I gave them tips and we swapped email addresses. We have stayed in touch ever since and one day I hope to invite Nelson to my country and to return the favour, showing him our beautiful land.

I've come to the end of my African Trilogy but this isn't the end of my story...

...I hope I have inspired you to go off and try it for yourselves...

And remember, "You have to have a dream, If you don't have a dream, how you gonna make a dream come true?!"

Cheers to Africa and your beautiful country! Asante Sana (thank you very much!)

La La Sa La Ma – Goodnight.

EPILOGUE

We all have a cross to bear, as the saying goes, and I am no exception. The final part of my book will take you into a dark place, some of you may have been there, to others it will seem like a horror story. All I can tell you is that it is true. It is the biggest mountain I have ever had to climb.

My Story - A Brief History Of Abuse.

I grew up in a house of extreme violence.

My first recollection of realising my life was abnormal was when I was being questioned by teachers about the bruises at the top of my legs.

We lived on a large estate in a remote village. Police, social workers and the truancy Officer were regular callers at our three-bedroom council house, which I shared with my mother, father, brother and handicapped sister.

My dad had two leather belts, a heavy-duty, thick one and a thinner one. Depending on his view of the severity of my behavior, my dad would administer punishment, using the belt he felt appropriately fitted the crime.

He would beat me, making me bend over the settee with my pants down, exposing myself, while he carried out the punishment. This continued for many years. I would scream with pain until he decided to stop beating me. He would say, if you don't stop crying, I will give you something to cry for. Afterwards, for the sake of self-preservation, I would internalize the pain, withhold tears and suffer in silence. My 'crimes' were eating a biscuit without permission, answering back and wetting the bed, which was ironic because the threat of violence from my dad was the cause of my bed wetting.

I was unable to concentrate at school because of the abusive treatment at home. I was singled out as a no-hoper, of low intelligence and beyond educating. In my class there was a special table nicknamed the "dougie table," where those considered beyond help were placed. It was supposed to give incentive to other pupils to work hard, or they too would be stigmatized and abandoned by the education system. Many years later I was to learn that I was dyslexic, not stupid.

My dad had been brought up in a family of sixteen children, he had lived off the land all his life and was determined we would do the same.

As a child my dad would take me and my brother out into the country, where we learned the skills of living off the land. When I reached the age of twelve or thirteen, my dad began taking me on my own. We would go for walks, collect scrap metal, steal from skips, gather vegetables and hunt with shotguns.

My dad would threaten my mother with his gun or

machete, the neighbours would hear the rows and would call the police. Sometimes my mother would scream out begging us to ring for help, but we never did, due to his threats and he made us go up to our bedrooms, where we had to listen as he continued to terrorise my mum.

The police would come on many occasions and I would hear them say they were not allowed to get involved in domestic arguments. She left him many times, but always returned. His jealous outbursts and heavy drinking left us in fear of our lives. On several occasions the police would remove the guns from the house, only to return them after a short period of time. He held a gun license and had shooting rights on one or two of the local farms.

I do have a few happy memories of my childhood, like when we would go out poaching, setting snares, hunting with ferrets and my pet dog, Sam. I loved being out in the countryside. However, my dad had a reputation for being a bully in our village, a violent man, who people were afraid of. Unfortunately I had to carry his name, which embarrassed me. Elliott Appleyard.

As time went by the walks became more frequent and usually excluded my brother, which meant my dad could spend more time alone with me. I could not understand why my dad chose me over my brother for these outings. However, the answer was about to become clear.

One day my dad lead me to a remote area behind a pipe manufacturer, Naylors. There was my dad, me and my pet dog Sam. Without warning, my dad pointed his gun at the dog and fired, killing Sam instantly. His reason was that the dog had fits and could not be trained for hunting and was of no use. I had never seen the dog have a fit. Suddenly he began to kiss me, not a peck on the cheek kiss, but a proper kiss, like boyfriend and girlfriend. He told me I was beautiful, that he loved me and I was special, mature beyond my years. I was the only one he could talk to, the only one who understood him. He said this was our secret and no one else could know. I sat there, shocked and confused, not knowing what to do. I didn't cry or show emotion.

Unlike the dog, my dad had trained me well.

To this day I recall my dad saying, "Who loves ya baby?"

I had to reply, "You do."

If I did not respond, he would repeat these words and I was forced to reply in order to keep the peace and please him.

He would say, "You'd better believe it." I would play along, but a feeling of sickness would engulf me, a feeling that still resonates in me to this day.

I told my mum about dad kissing me and begged her not to say anything, afraid of my dad's reaction and of his violence, which would surely follow. Eventually, and unbeknownst to me, she told the social services and two social workers came to my school and questioned me about my dad. I told them he was kissing me properly, not like a father and daughter kiss. When I went home from school that day, mum talked about leaving dad and taking me with her.

The next day we left, but my brother and sister remained at the house. Mum took me to a house in Penistone to stay with people she had just met over the CB radio. We had to sleep on a mattress on bare floorboards. I knew nobody and missed my brother and sister. Nothing more was mentioned about my dad kissing me and because I was occupied with starting a new school and trying to make friends, I guess I forgot about it.

We eventually were evicted and moved on to stay with another lady and her family where we shared bunk beds in a single room. Things got tough between mum and myself, to the extent that she took an overdose in front of me, one of many attempts at suicide that I had witnessed. Her actions didn't help at a time when I was craving stability and feeling insecure.

My mum went out a lot, enjoying her new found freedom, but left me on my own. I was thirteen at this stage. Eventually my dad made contact with me and we met up in Barnsley market. He seemed to be a normal dad and he bought me a pair of jeans. My mum often said to me, "What a price you paid for a pair of jeans!" This sickens me as I didn't know what I would be getting myself into but she obviously did.

When I decided to go back to live with my dad, it seemed a welcome relief from the uncertainty, instability and discomfort of living with strangers and from feeling vulnerable because mum was hardly around.

After moving back to my dad's, a social worker, Mr Sykes, came to see me at our house. He made me feel like I had done something wrong for leaving my mum.

Mr Sykes told me, "Because you have lived with your mum and now you've come back to live with your dad, it's obvious you can't make up your mind who you want to live with."

He continued, "If you change your mind again, you will go into a children's home."

I was scared and have never forgotten the social worker's harsh words that day. I had seen how my poor sister had suffered in a children's home. Following this, dad went to the court and got custody of me and my brother. My sister went to live with my mum.

Not long after this my dad started play fighting and giving me massive love bites, so boys of my own age wouldn't' be interested in me and would think that I was a slag. I felt ashamed and dare not tell anybody that it was my dad who had given me the love bites.

My dad had gone away on a hunting trip to America and we were being looked after by my aunty Hilda. While he was away, my brother and I threw a party which caused some damage. My dad was extremely angry about the party and that my mum had taken half the furniture while he was gone. I was so scared of him beating me that I cut my wrist. He said it wasn't that bad and that I wouldn't' need to go to hospital and he bandaged my wrist himself and said I was mentally unstable and shouldn't be left alone. He said I would have to sleep in his bed tonight. I thought he was just being caring and I was happy that he wasn't angry anymore and he cuddled up to me before I went to sleep.

He woke me up stroking my tummy and then he raped me for the first time.

Afterwards, I asked my dad, "What would granddad say about what you just did?"

He replied, "Don't worry, he believed the same as me, that fathers should break their daughters in, like the Indians do." He was referring to Native American Indians and, at the time, I did not know any different and didn't question it.

The rapes happened nearly every day for about two years. I used to lay in bed at night, curled up in the foetal position, praying that when he came home from the pub he would go past my room and leave me alone. I would pretend to be asleep but he would come in and take me by my arm and lead me to his room. I would have to keep quiet so that my brother would not hear. I thought that if he found out, there would be a massive fallout and we would both end up in a children's home.

I felt it was my responsibility to keep what family we had left together. My dad made me play the role of a wife and kept me off school a lot. He put my mum's engagement ring on my finger; he then told me that I should call him Sam and not dad. This was a name I'd never heard before, but he told me it was his nickname from his younger days.

My dad took me and my brother for a tattoo, mine saying *Sam and Caz*, with a rose in-between on my shoulder and my brothers saying *Sam and Paul* with the same rose, on his forearm. My dad had a swallow tattooed on his neck at the same time. I was thirteen and my brother was twelve.

It took six painful years to have the tattoo removed and I still carry the scar.

I would have to cook and if it wasn't up to my mum's standard, he would throw the hot pan against the wall. Through the day I was responsible for all the domestic chores around the house. He would come home and have sex with me like a wife. He always used a condom. He kept them in a draw at the side of his bed. He could not risk me getting pregnant and exposing him to the world. He said if I got pregnant, the baby would be an albino. At one stage, I thought I was pregnant and I was scared, I went to my mum's house for help and she took me for a pregnancy test. She asked me who the father was and I told her just a boy I was seeing. I still daren't tell her about my dad raping me because I was afraid of the consequences and the threat of being placed in a children's home if I went back to live with mum.

Thank god I wasn't pregnant.

My dad would tell me that it was normal for a father and daughter to live like man and wife, as he had said that he had several friends who did so and were very happy. I was confused and didn't know what to think or feel.

He would still say, "Who loves ya baby?"

I would have to reply, "You do."

I played along with the role of being a happy housewife for the sake of self-preservation and the family's, but I was never happy: I was frightened of him.

I played the part so well, that I believe, in his sick mind, he thought I was actually happy. It got to the stage where I would pretend to enjoy sex so the ordeal would be over quicker.

One lunch time he came home and wanted sex. He made me lay me down in front of the roaring fire. Whilst he was raping me, my leg was burning. I stood it for as long as I could, thinking it would be over soon, but it got too painful.

I had to say, "My leg's burning."

He became very angry and said I was only saying that because I didn't want to do it.

Afraid of what he would do to me, I pleaded with him and said, "No, I do."

He often made me have oral sex with him as well and he stank. He was filthy.

I was trapped and had nowhere to go.

After two years of sexual abuse and being called pathetic, I couldn't take any more and I finally plucked up the courage to leave. I went to my mum's house and told her about the abuse I had suffered, the rapes and the sexual abuse my dad had put me through.

Immediately mum contacted my dad.

"Carol's with me and she's told me everything."

He replied, "You can't prove a thing."

I didn't go to the police straight away because I felt ashamed and believed I was partly to blame. I thought I could forget about it and just get on with my life, but I couldn't.

It was about a week later when I eventually built up enough courage and my mum took me to the police station where I made a seventeen page statement. The next day I underwent internal forensic tests at Huddersfield police station. The swabs showed I was bleeding internally and forensic officers had me jumping up and down over blotting paper. The whole process was another violation.

My dad had always been careful to use condoms, so there was a lack of forensic evidence. This made any possibility of prosecution highly unlikely. Added to this, my dad later made a statement to the police stating that I had a reputation for sleeping around and was sexually active with a number of boys. This was completely untrue but it was his word against mine. I had never had the opportunity to go out with other boys due to my dad's possessiveness towards me and jealousy.

My brother witnessed my dad's inappropriate behaviour towards me, seeing him full-on snogging me and seeing us in bed together on a Saturday morning. Neighbours had also seen him holding hands with me and acting like a boyfriend with a girlfriend.

After the time I had made my statement (when I was fifteen), at Penitstone police station, the police said that my thirteen year old brother would be classed as a juvenile witness, so his evidence could not be used in court. I have since been told that this was incorrect, and his testimony would have been admissible. The police had questioned my dad but he denied everything. My brother heard him telling his new wife that I came on to him and when he rejected my advances, I came up with the allegations of my father's constant sexual abuse.

A policeman warned me that if the case went to court, I would be made out to be the biggest liar in the courtroom and my sexual history would be called into question. The policeman also said that my character would be blackened and I would be dragged through the mud.

The officer asked, "Could you handle that?"

I decided, *no I couldn't*.

I felt ashamed that at age thirteen, I was not a virgin. I had slept with someone in the house in Penistone where I had been lodging. He was about nineteen and I had craved affection. I didn't want him to get into trouble if it came out in court.

I was told that because my case had not reached the Crown Prosecution Service, it could be investigated again in the future when my brother was older. Whereas, if it *had* gone to court and been tried and thrown out, there would be no chance of re-opening the case. I still had hope that my dad would be brought to justice.

However, about ten years ago, I went back to the police and told them I wanted to report a case of historical child sex abuse. They put me in touch with the child protection unit. It was at this time that I found out from D.I. Sonia Miller, that because my case had already been investigated back in 1984 and because the statement and forensic evidence had since been lost, the case was now closed and couldn't be re-opened. I was outraged and upset at the injustice of them having lost my evidence and then saying the case had been fully investigated, when I knew it hadn't.

I pleaded with D.I. Sonia Miller over the phone to let me compile a new statement and she agreed. I thought I would have to go to the police station to make new statements but she told me to do it at home. I had written a few pages and wanted to know if what I was writing was what she required. I phoned her and she came out to my home. I showed her my draft statement and she took it away to read. She rang me back, as promised, but to my astonishment, she told me she had already presented it to the CPS. She knew it was incomplete, so it was no surprise, then, that it was rejected and I was told they would not look at my case again.

Despite feeling that I was being fobbed off and that I was not believed, I could not let it go. I felt like I needed justice. Therefore, five years later I made another attempt to open the case, speaking to the same D.I. Sonia Miller from the Child Protection Unit. This time she told me that because they had lost the statements and forensic evidence, unless another victim came forward, the case would not be re-opened. I knew that my cousin had been raped many times by my dad in his van on the way home after baby-sitting for us. She had been about thirteen. I tracked my cousin down and found that she had bi-polar disorder and had been to court on behalf of a friend who had been raped. The case had been thrown out and she said there was no way she was going to put herself through that again. She was still afraid of my dad, as well. The door was closed on me, yet again.

This did not stop me trying again in 2014, but to no avail once again. I went into the police station and told them I wanted to report an historical child sexual abuse. They asked if it was me, and I replied that it was.

I waited five hours to see somebody and they finally took a statement from me, which was passed to D.I. Sonia Miller who said it could not be classed as evidence. She asked me for a list of witnesses and any other evidence I had, she wanted fresh evidence. I gave her the names of my mum and brother and a neighbour and also information about my social worker and police involvement with my dad.

D.I. Sonia Miller telephoned my brother and asked him if he had witnessed any inappropriate behaviour by my father. He told her that he had seen my father kissing me properly and had seen us in his bed together. My brother told her that he has no contact with my dad and would never let his three children anywhere near him.

He said, "Once a paedophile, always a paedophile!"

The D.I. said this was not adequate evidence, as her daughter kisses and gets into bed with her husband. A letter which my mother had written to me contained evidence that she knew I was being abused, but this new evidence was rejected by the police as well.

The West Yorkshire Police say there is insufficient evidence but how do they know until they properly investigate? My Mum and brother had never been asked to make a statement once!

My original seventeen page statement, which they told me had been lost, has, in actual fact, been burnt, according to one of D.I. Sonia Miller's colleagues, along with other historical child sex abuse cases from that era.

Unbelievably, D.I. Millar says there is no record of intervention by social services in our family, despite me being able to name social workers and despite my sister being in a children's home. There is also no record of police intervention concerning domestic violence with my father and no record of him having his guns confiscated. There was not even a record of him beating my uncle Ken to a pulp, injuring him so badly that he had to be revived by paramedics.

I had undergone years of counselling but still couldn't find peace or closure. I tried to achieve this eight years ago on Father's Day, by going to his house to say I forgave him. That day I had been to my church and the strength of my faith made me realise that I should not fear a coward, but pity him. When I challenged him about the abuse, he refused to talk about it.

I said to him, "I thought you might be sorry for what you did to me."

He avoided my eyes, looked away and spoke, almost inaudibly, "Sorry".

I knew he didn't mean it. He was simply trying to keep the peace because his wife was in the next room. If she had heard him say sorry, it would have been an admission of his guilt.

In 2012 I watched a programme called Newsnight, which talked about how incest was rife in the UK. Boys and girls were being abused in the UK and were not being listened to. This resonated deeply within me, I could relate to feeling the pain and fear that was so hard to bare.

I felt I needed to tell my story, even though I have been failed so many times, as have so many other victims, I still have to go on trying to find healing along my life's journey. Speaking up about my past is part of the process.

Why should I have to keep silent? Where is the justice?

As a child I was groomed and abused and it was not an isolated incident. It was perpetrated over a number of years by my father, Elliott Appleyard. It took me years to understand that I was not to blame: I was a victim.

The social workers involved knew our family well, but throughout all their intervention they failed to protect me. West Yorkshire Constabulary had lost the evidence that might have brought my father to justice. But he is still out there, able to abuse other vulnerable children. The police would do well to scrutinise their attitude towards victims, both current and historical, especially in light of the recent revelations about celebrities, politicians and other high-powered people involved in child sexual abuse. There are so many children who are afraid to speak up, who are scared of not being believed and who fear the justice system is likely to fail them. If we stand together we can overcome.

In life we encounter many mountains, we are overwhelmed by them. The choice is to fear them or conquer them. Throughout my life I have chosen to do the latter. My strength and love goes out to you all.

X

ABOUT THE AUTHOR

Carol Higgins (45) grew up in a dysfunctional and abusive family in Denby Dale, W. Yorks, and as a result left school with no qualifications.

Working in a sewing factory for eight years before marrying and having two children, Carol helped her ex-husband build a successful business.

Divorced and bringing up two children alone, Carol gave her spare time to work with the elderly and children in schools and as a youth worker, soon enrolling on adult education courses.

Until as recently as 2014, Carol did not know that she was dyslexic, a diagnosis that helped Carol to realise why she had struggled all of her life, particularly in school, work and college.

Carol lives in Ackworth, Yorkshire, with her grown up son and daughter, Jake (21) and Ella (17), where she is a keen fundraiser for numerous charities.

Made in the USA
Charleston, SC
19 April 2015